Don't Make Me Laugh!

THE NEW WINDMILL BOOK OF HUMOROUS STORIES

EDITED BY DAVID KITCHEN

Heinemann
New Windmills

Heinemann Educational Publishers
Halley Court, Jordan Hill, Oxford OX2 8EJ
a division of Reed Educational & Professional Publishing Ltd

OXFORD   MELBOURNE   AUCKLAND
JOHANNESBURG   BLANTYRE   GABORONE
IBADAN   PORTSMOUTH (NH) USA   CHICAGO

2002 2001 2000
10 9 8 7 6 5

ISBN 0 435 12497 8

Acknowledgements
A big thank you to all the students at Llantarnam School in Cwmbran who helped to make this
book possible.

The editor and publisher wish to thank the following for permission
to use copyright material:
Penguin Books Australia Ltd for 'Licked' from *Unbearable!* and 'Wunderpants' from *Unreal!* by
Paul Jennings, pp1, 80; David Higham Associates for 'You Don't Look Very Poorly' from
Crummy Mummy and Me by Anne Fine, published by Penguin, p7; David Higham Associates
Limited for 'Swalk' by Sam McBratney © Sam McBratney 1994, from *In Between*, edited by
Miriam Hodgson, published by Methuen, p17; Reed Books for 'Uninvited Ghosts' by Penelope
Lively from *Frank and Polly Muir's Big Dipper*, published by William Heinemann, 1981, p28; 'A
Ghost of One's Own' reproduced with permission of Curtis Brown Ltd, London, on behalf of
Ursula Moray Williams. Copyright Ursula Moray Williams, p53; 'Dog's Dinner' © 1998 Lynne
Hackles, and reproduced by permission of the author and Laurence Pollinger Limited, p69;
'Cuts' © 1996, 1998 Russell Hoban by permission of David Higham Associates. An earlier
version of 'Cuts' appeared in *Metropolitan* Magazine in 1996, p76; 'Tama Gotcher' © 1998
Robert Dawson, and reproduced by permission of the author and Laurence Pollinger Limited,
p94; Random House for 'The Dolls' from *The Daydreamer* by Ian McEwan, published by
Jonathan Cape, p100; 'A Prawn in the Game' © 1998 Elaine Sishton, and reproduced by
permission of the author and Laurence Pollinger Limited, p111; Reed Books for 'QWERTYUIOP'
from *Ghostly Companions* by Vivien Alcock. Copyright © 1984 by Vivien Alcock, published by
Methuen Children's Books Ltd, 1984, p118; David Higham Associates for 'William Darling' from
Shark and Chips and Other Stories by Anne Fine, published by Puffin, p133; 'The Bakerloo Flea'
reprinted by permission of The Peters Fraser and Dunlop Group Limited on behalf of: Michael
Rosen © Michael Rosen, p143; 'The Stowaways' reprinted by permission of The Peters Fraser
and Dunlop Group Limited on behalf of: Roger McGough © Roger McGough, p152.

Cover design by The Point
Image by Photo Disc Europe Ltd
Typeset by 🗚 Tek-Art, Croydon, Surrey
Printed and bound in the United Kingdom by Clays Ltd, St Ives plc

Contents

Introduction

We spent ages on it. Firstly, there was the finding of the stories: hundreds of them. Secondly, there was the business of thinning them down to a manageable number. That was easier said than done. Then came student choice time. Hundreds of students each read dozens of stories during a term of reading. And every time someone read a story they voted for or against it.

The result is this book which collects together the very best of the bunch. The stories include the unlikely, the bizarre, the embarrassing and the plain revolting. Michael Rosen takes us on the trail of an over-sized underground flea. Ursula Moray Williams faces up to the problems of sticking the family ghost in a basket for a bus journey. Vivien Alcock addresses the challenge of a typewriter which answers back.

There doesn't seem to be any formula that makes a story amusing. Sometimes we were laughing because we recognized people in stories behaving like people we knew. On other occasions, we were entertained by things that were so far from real life, we wondered how the writer had come up with the idea. Many of the stories were popular because they held surprises. In some of them, the pleasure was in reading about what we guessed was going to happen and seeing how it worked out.

We have thoroughly enjoyed putting this collection together and are certain that everyone will find something in it to make them laugh.

David Kitchen

Licked
Paul Jennings

Tomorrow when Dad calms down I'll own up. Tell him the truth. He might laugh. He might cry. He might strangle me. But I have to put him out of his misery.

I like my dad. He takes me fishing. He gives me arm wrestles in front of the fire on cold nights. He plays Scrabble instead of watching the news. He tries practical jokes on me. And he keeps his promises. Always.

But he has two faults. Bad faults. One is to do with flies. He can't stand them. If there's a fly in the room he has to kill it. He won't use fly spray because of the ozone layer so he chases them with a fly swat. He races around the house swiping and swatting like a mad thing. He won't stop until the fly is flat. Squashed. Squished – sometimes still squirming on the end of the fly swat.

He's a dead-eye shot. He hardly ever misses. When his old fly swat was almost worn out I bought him a nice new yellow one for his birthday. It wasn't yellow for long. It soon had bits of fly smeared all over it.

It's funny the different colours that squashed flies have inside them. Mostly it is black or brown. But often there are streaks of runny red stuff and sometimes bits of blue. The wings flash like diamonds if you hold them up to the light. But mostly the wings fall off unless they are stuck to the swat with a bit of squashed innards.

Chasing flies is Dad's first fault. His second one is table manners. He is mad about manners.

And it is always my manners that are the matter.

'Andrew,' he says. 'Don't put your elbows on the table.'

'Don't talk with your mouth full.'

'Don't lick your fingers.'

'Don't dunk your biscuit in the coffee.'

This is the way he goes on every meal time. He has a thing about flies and a thing about manners.

Anyway, to get back to the story. One day Dad is peeling the potatoes for tea. I am looking for my fifty cents that rolled under the table about a week ago. Mum is cutting up the cabbage and talking to Dad. They do not know that I am there. It is a very important meal because Dad's boss, Mr Spinks, is coming for tea. Dad never stops going on about my manners when someone comes for tea.

'You should stop picking on Andrew at tea time,' says Mum.

'I don't,' says Dad.

'Yes you do,' says Mum. 'It's always "don't do this, don't do that." You'll give the boy a complex.'

I have never heard of a complex before but I guess that it is something awful like pimples.

'Tonight,' says Mum. 'I want you to go for the whole meal without telling Andrew off once.'

'Easy,' says Dad.

'Try hard,' says Mum. 'Promise me that you won't get cross with him.'

Dad looks at her for a long time. 'Okay,' he says. 'It's a deal. I won't say one thing about his manners. But you're not allowed to either. What's good for me is good for you.'

'Shake,' says Mum. They shake hands and laugh.

I find the fifty cents and sneak out. I take a walk down the street to spend it before tea. Dad has promised not to tell me off at tea time. I think about how I can make him crack. It should be easy. I will slurp my soup. He hates that. He will tell me off. He might even yell. I just know that he can't go for the whole meal without going crook. 'This is going to be fun,' I say to myself.

That night Mum sets the table with the new tablecloth. And the best knives and forks. And the plates that I am not allowed to touch. She puts out serviettes in little rings. All of this means that it is an important meal. We don't usually use serviettes.

Mr Spinks comes in his best suit. He wears gold glasses and he frowns a lot. I can tell that he doesn't like children. You can always tell when adults don't like kids. They smile at you with their lips but not with their eyes.

Anyway, we sit down to tea. I put my secret weapon on the floor under the table. I'm sure that I can make Dad crack without using it. But it is there if all else fails.

The first course is soup and bread rolls. I make loud slurping noises with the soup. No one says anything about it. I make the slurping noises longer and louder. They go on and on and on. It sounds like someone has pulled the plug out of the bath. Dad clears his throat but doesn't say anything.

I try something different. I dip my bread in the soup and make it soggy. Then I hold it high above my head and drop it down into my mouth. I catch it with a loud slopping noise. I try again with an even bigger bit. This time I miss my mouth and the bit of soupy bread hits me in the eye.

Nothing is said. Dad looks at me. Mum looks at me. Mr Spinks tries not to look at me. They are talking about how Dad might get a promotion at work. They are pretending that I am not revolting.

The next course is chicken. Dad will crack over the chicken. He'll say something. He hates me picking up the bones.

The chicken is served. 'I've got the chicken's bottom,' I say in a loud voice.

Dad glares at me but he doesn't answer. I pick up the chicken and start stuffing it into my mouth with my fingers. I grab a roast potato and break it in half. I dip my fingers into the margarine and put some on the potato. It runs all over the place.

I have never seen anyone look as mad as the way Dad looks at me. He glares. He stares. He clears his throat. But still he doesn't crack. What a man. Nothing can make him break his promise.

I snap a chicken bone in half and suck out the middle. It is hollow and I can see right through it. I suck and slurp and swallow. Dad is going red in the face. Little veins are standing out on his nose. But still he does not crack.

The last course is baked apple and custard. I will get him with that. Mr Spinks has stopped talking about Dad's promotion. He is discussing something about discipline. About setting limits. About insisting on standards. Something like that. I put the hollow bone into the custard and use it like a straw. I suck the custard up the hollow chicken bone.

Dad clears his throat. He is very red in the face. 'Andrew,' he says.

He is going to crack. I have won.

'Yes,' I say through a mouth full of custard.

'Nothing,' he mumbles.

Dad is terrific. He is under enormous pressure but still he keeps his cool. There is only one thing left to do. I take out my secret weapon.

I place the yellow fly swat on the table next to my knife.

Everyone looks at it lying there on the white tablecloth. They stare and stare and stare. But nothing is said.

I pick up the fly swat and start to lick it. I lick it like an ice cream. A bit of chewy, brown goo comes off on my tongue. I swallow it quickly. Then I crunch a bit of crispy, black stuff.

Mr Spinks rushes out to the kitchen. I can hear him being sick in the kitchen sink.

Dad stands up. It is too much for him. He cracks. 'Aaaaaagh,' he screams. He charges at me with hands held out like claws.

I run for it. I run down to my room and lock the door. Dad yells and shouts. He kicks and screams. But I lie low.

Tomorrow, when he calms down, I'll own up. I'll tell him how I went down the street and bought a new fly swat for fifty cents. I'll tell him about the currants and little bits of licorice that I smeared on the fly swat.

I mean, I wouldn't really eat dead flies. Not unless it was for something important anyway.

You Don't Look Very Poorly
Adapted from *Crummy Mummy and Me*
Anne Fine

You don't exactly *ask* to get sick, do you? I mean, you don't go round *inviting* germs and viruses to move in and do their worst to your body. You don't actually *apply* for trembling legs and feeling shivery, and a head that's had a miniature steel band practising for a carnival in it all night.

And if you should happen to mention to your own mother that you feel absolutely terrible, you would expect a bit of sympathy, wouldn't you?

I wouldn't. Not any more.

'You don't *look* very poorly.'

That's what she said. And she said it suspiciously, too, as if I was one of those people who's always making excuses to stay off school and spend the day wrapped in a downie on the sofa watching *Bagpuss* and *Playschool* and *Pebble Mill at One*.

'Well, I feel absolutely rotten.'

'You don't look it.'

'I'm sorry!' I snapped. (I was getting pretty cross.) 'Sorry I can't manage a bright-green face for you! Or purple spots on my belly! Or all my hair falling out! But I feel rotten just the same!'

And I burst into tears.

(Now that's not like me.)

'Now that's not like you,' said Mum, sounding sympathetic at last. 'You must be a little bit off today.'

'I am not *off*,' I snarled through my tears. 'I'm not leftover milk. Or rotten fish.'

'There, there,' Mum soothed. 'Don't fret, Minna. Don't get upset. You just hop straight back up those stairs like a good poppet, and in a minute I'll bring something nice up on a tray, and you can have a quiet day in bed, with Mum looking after you until you feel better.'

That was a bit more like it, as I think you'll agree. So I stopped snivelling and went back to bed. I didn't exactly hop straight back up those stairs because I was feeling so crummy and weak I could barely drag myself up hanging on to the banisters; but I got up somehow, and put on my dressing-gown and buttoned it right up to the top to keep my chest warm, and plumped up my pillows so I could sit comfortably, and switched on my little plastic frog reading-lamp, and folded my hands in my lap, and I waited.

And I waited.

And I waited.

(In case you're wondering, I was waiting for Mum to bring me up something nice on a tray and look after me until I felt better.)

She never came.

Oh, I'm sure that she *meant* to come. I'm sure she had every intention of coming. I'm sure it wasn't her fault the milkman came and needed paying, and it took time to work out what she owed because he'd been away for two weeks on his holiday in Torremolinos.

And I'm sure it wasn't Mum's fault that he took the opportunity to park his crate of bottles down on the doorstep and tell her all about the way some sneaky people always bagged the best pool-loungers by creeping down at dead of night and dropping their swimming towels over them; and how his wife's knees burned and peeled but none of the rest of her, even though all of her was out in the sun for the same amount of time; and how his daughter Meryl came home to her job at the

Halifax with a broken heart because of some fellow called Miguel Angel Gippini Lopez de Rego, who danced like a fury but turned out to be engaged to a Spanish girl working in Barcelona.

Oh, it wasn't Mum's fault that she had to listen to all that before she could get away to bring me up something nice on a tray and look after me until I was better. But I could hear them talking clearly enough on the doorstep. And I don't actually recall hearing her say firmly but politely: 'Excuse me, Mr Hooper, but Minna's in bed feeling terrible, and I must get back upstairs, so I'll listen to all the rest tomorrow.' I heard quite a bit; but I didn't hear that.

As soon as the milkman had chinked off next door, I thought I heard Mum making for the bottom of the stairs. But she never got there.

'YeeeeoooooowwwwwwwaaaaaAAAAAAAAAEEEEEWWW!'

You guessed it. My baby sister woke up.

And I suppose it wasn't Mum's fault that Miranda needed her nappy changing. And that there weren't any dry ones because we don't have a tumble-drier and it had been raining for three solid days. And Mum had forgotten to pick up another packet of disposables last time she practically *swam* down to the shops.

So Mum decided the simplest thing would be to park Miranda in the playpen where little accidents don't matter. It wasn't her fault it took for ever to drag it out of the cupboard because she had dumped my sledge, and the dress-up box, and all the empty jars she's saving for Gran, right in front of it. Or that she had to fetch the damp nappies off the line and drape them over the rack in the kitchen.

And I suppose it's understandable that while she was shaking out the damp nappies, she should glance out of the window at the grey skies and think about nipping

down to the launderette with the rest of the washing and
handing it to Mrs Hajee to do in the machines, since it
really didn't look as if it would ever stop raining.

So I suppose it does make sense that the very next
thing I heard on my quiet day in bed was Mum bellowing
up the stairs: 'Minna! *Minna!* Look after the baby
for a few minutes, will you, while I nip down to the
launderette? She's perfectly happy in her playpen with
her toys. Just come down if she starts to squawk.'

Fine. Lovely. Sure. Here am I, feeling really terrible and
looking forward to something nice on a tray and being
looked after until I feel better, and suddenly I'm looking
after the baby! Fine. Lovely. Sure.

To be quite fair to Mum, she didn't stay out any longer
than was absolutely necessary. There was the launderette,
of course. And then she had to get the disposable nappies
or Miranda would have had to spend the whole morning
sitting on her cold bottom in the playpen, waiting for
the ones in the kitchen to dry. And while she was in the
supermarket she did pick up bread, and a quarter of
sliced ham, and a few oranges and a couple of other
things, making too many to get through the quick
checkout. And there were really long queues at all the
others because it was pension-day morning. And she did
just pop into the newsagent's on her way home as well.
And, yes, she did stop on the corner for a second, but that
was just to be polite to the Lollipop Lady who told her
that, whatever it was I'd got, there was a lot of it about,
and Mum ought to be really careful or she'd come down
with it as well.

And then she came straight home. She *says* she was
out for no more than five minutes at the very most. But
I've a watch, so I know better.

Then, at last, she came up to my room. She had
Miranda tucked under one arm, all bare bottom and

wriggles, and she was carrying a tray really high in the air, practically above her head, so my sister couldn't upset it with all her flailing arms and legs. It was so high I couldn't see what was on it from the bed.

'I don't know how these nurses do it,' said Mum. 'They should have medals pinned on their chests, not watches.'

I looked at mine. It was exactly half-past ten. (I fell sick at 8.23.)

'If you were a nurse,' I said, 'you would have got the sack two hours ago.'

'I'd like to see you do any better,' she snapped back, sharpish.

'I bet I would,' I told her. 'I bet if *you* were sick, it wouldn't take *me* two whole hours to bring you something nice on a tray.'

'I should wait till you see what there is on the tray before you start grumbling,' Mum warned. And then she lowered it on to the bed in front of me.

And there was a cup of very milky coffee with bubbles on top in my favourite fat china bear mug, and a huge orange cut into the thinnest possible circular slices, just how I like it when I want to nibble at the peel as well. And a chocolate-biscuit bar and the latest *Beano* and *Dandy*, and a pack of twenty brand-new fine-tipped felt pens.

I felt dead guilty for being so grumpy.

'I'm sorry I said you'd get the sack as a nurse.'

'Oh, that's all right,' Mum answered cheerfully. She flipped Miranda over and put a nappy on her before there was trouble and even more laundry. 'It's a well-known fact that it's even harder to be a good patient than a good nurse.'

'Is that true?'

'Certainly.'

And then, with my baby sister safe at last, Mum sat down on my bed and took a break.

I thought about what she said quite a lot while I was getting better. As I sipped my coffee, and nibbled my orange circles, and read my *Beano*, and made my chocolate biscuit last as long as I could while I was drawing with my brand-new felt pens, I wondered what sort of patient Mum would make. She isn't famous in this house for long-suffering meekness or sunny patience.

And I wondered what sort of nurse I'd make – sensitive, deft, unflappable, efficient . . .

I'd no idea I would find out so soon.

It was only two days later, on Saturday morning, that Mum leaned over the banisters and called down: 'Minna, I feel just awful. Awful.'

'You don't *look* very poorly.'

(I didn't mean it that way. It just popped out.)

You'd have thought I was trying to suggest she was faking.

'I may not *look* it, but I *am*,' she snapped. 'I feel as if I've been left out all night in the rain, and my bones have gone soggy, and hundreds of spiteful little men with steel boots are holding a stamping competition in my brain.'

Personally, even without the Lollipop Lady saying there was a lot of it about, I would have recognized the symptoms at once.

I was determined to show Mum what proper nursing ought to be.

'You go straight back to bed,' I ordered. 'I'll take care of you, and everything else. You tuck yourself in comfortably, and I'll bring up something nice on a tray.'

Mum swayed a little against the banisters. She did look pale.

'You are an angel, Minna,' she said faintly. And wrapping her shiny black skull-and-crossbones dressing-gown more closely around her string-vest nightie, she staggered back into the bedroom.

I don't have to tell you about my plan, do I? You'll already have guessed. Yes, I was going to rush back into the kitchen and spread a tray with lovely, tempting treats for an invalid's breakfast – treats like a cup of tea made just the way Mum really likes it, golden-pale, not that lovely, thick, murky, dark sludge favoured by me and Gran. (We joke that Mum's tea is too weak to crawl out of the pot.) And I was going to pick a tiny posy of flowers from the garden, and arrange them in one of the pretty china egg-cups.

And I was going to bring the tray up without delay.

Guess what went wrong first. No, don't bother. I'll tell you. First, I locked myself out. Honestly. Me, Minna. The only one in the house who *never* does it. I did it. I was so keen to get my tray arranged that I stepped out of the back door into the garden to find the flowers without checking the latch.

Clunk!

The moment I heard the door close behind me, I realized. I could have kicked myself in the shins. I picked my way around to the front, just on the off-chance that the front door was unlocked. But I knew it wouldn't be, and of course it wasn't.

I stood there, thinking. I had two choices. I could ring the doorbell and drag poor, shaking, deathly pale Mum from her bed of sickness and down the stairs to let me in; or I could slip next door to old Mrs Pitopoulos, ring her bell instead, and ask to borrow the spare key to our house she keeps for emergencies in an old cocoa-tin under her sink.

I knew which a good nurse would do. I went next door and rang the bell.

No answer.

I rang again.

Still no answer.

Suddenly I noticed a faint scrabbling overhead. I looked up, and there was Mrs Pitopoulos in her quilted dressing-gown, fighting the stiff window-catch with her arthritic fingers.

She couldn't budge it, so she just beckoned me inside the house.

I tried the front door. It was locked. I went round the back, and that door opened. I picked my way through the furry sea of all her pet cats rubbing their arched backs against my legs, so pleased to see me, and went upstairs.

Mrs Pitopoulos was sitting on the edge of her bed. Her face looked like a wrinkled sack, and her wig was all crooked.

'You look very poorly,' I told her.

I couldn't help it. It just popped out.

'Oh, Minna,' she said. 'I feel terrible, terrible. My legs are rubber, and there are red-hot nails in my head.'

'I've had that,' I said. 'Mum's got it now. The Lollipop Lady says that there's lots of it about.'

When she heard this, Mrs Pitopoulos began to look distinctly better. Maybe when you're that age and you get sick, you think whatever it is has come to get you. At any rate, she tugged her wig round on her head, and even the wrinkles seemed to flatten out a bit.

'Minna,' she said. 'Would you do me a great favour, and feed my hungry cats?'

'What about you?' I said. 'Have you had anything this morning?'

'Oh I'm not hungry,' Mrs Pitopoulos declared.

But then she cocked her head on one side, and wondered about it. And then she added: 'Maybe I do feel just a little bit peckish. Yesterday my sister brought me all these lovely things: new-laid brown speckled eggs and home-made bread and a tiny pot of fresh strawberry jam. But what I'd really like is . . . ' (Her eyes were gleaming, and she looked miles better.) 'What I'd really like is a bowl of Heinz tomato soup with bits of white bread floating on the top.'

Even I can cook that.

And so I did. And fed her cats. And she was so pleased when I brought the soup up to her on a tray that she pressed on me all the little gifts her sister had brought round the day before: the new-laid brown speckled eggs and home-made bread and tiny pot of fresh strawberry jam – oh, and the door-key of course.

Mum was astonished when I brought the tray up. I thought she must have been asleep. She looked as if she had been dozing. She heaved herself upright against the pillows, and I laid the tray down on her knees.

'Minna!' she cried. 'Oh, how lovely! Look at the flowers!'

'Wait till you've tasted the food,' I said.

I could tell that she didn't really feel much like eating. But she was determined not to hurt my feelings, so she reached out and took one of the strips of hot buttered toast made from the home-made bread.

She nibbled the crust politely.

'Delicious,' she said. And then, 'Mmm. *Delicious*.'

She couldn't help dipping the next strip of toast into the new-laid brown speckled soft-boiled egg.

'Mmmm!' she cried. 'This is *wonderful*.'

After the egg was eaten, she still had two strips of toast left. She spread one with the fresh strawberry jam, and off she went again.

'Mmmm! *Marvellous!*'

She went into raptures over the golden-pale tea. (I reckoned I'd have a battle ever forcing her back to medium-brown, when she felt well again.) And then she leaned back against the pillows, smiling.

She looked a lot better.

'I'll bring you some more, if you'd like it,' I offered.

'You are the *very best nurse*,' Mum declared. 'You managed all this, and so quickly too!'

Now I was sure she'd been dozing. I'd taken *ages*.

'You're the *very best patient*,' I returned the compliment. 'You don't notice what's going on, and how long it takes!'

'Silly,' she said, and snuggled back under the bedcovers.

I think she must have thought I was joking.

SWALK
Sam McBratney

The card he was expecting arrived a day early. Monty Quayle found it waiting for him when he got home from school on the thirteenth of February. His first impulse was to chuck it on the fire there and then and be done with it, for he had no time for this slushy, lovey-dovey St Valentine's Day nonsense; but he didn't do that. Perhaps the sheer size of the white envelope appealed to his sense of curiosity. It seemed a good deal too large for his letterbox.

'Who's your admirer, then?' his mother asked slyly as she passed through the kitchen trailing coffee fumes.

'Some twit of a girl,' he said.

'In your form?'

'How do I know?' said Monty, heading smartly for the privacy of his own room. His mother had had two questions and two answers on this subject – more than she had a right to expect.

Actually he had a pretty good idea who was torturing him in this way. In yesterday's French class Gail Summers and Anne Clarke had informed him that he would be receiving a valentine card on February the fourteenth.

'How do you know?' he'd asked in all innocence.

'A wee bird told us,' they said, adding that this card would have the French word for 'love' on it. 'L'amour,' they said, and started to laugh until Anne Clarke sounded like a camel.

In the peace and quiet of his own room Monty examined the uninvited card with as much generosity of spirit as he could muster. One of the giant red hearts on the front had a jagged split running through it, and it sickened him, that broken heart. Your heart was a thumping big muscle in the middle of your chest, it couldn't snap in two like a cheese and onion crisp and how people could ignore a simple fact like that was beyond his understanding. 'My heart longs for you,' said one of the lines inside. Hearts couldn't long for anything, they were for pumping blood and you might as well long for somebody with your left kidney. 'My brain longs for you' would be better. Not that he wanted Gail Summers' or Anne Clarke's brain to long for him either, but at least it would make sense from a biological point of view.

The whole card was a mass of scrawled verses which were so awful that he couldn't stop reading them. What could one say about:

>'Roses are red,
>Violets are blue,
>If I had three feet,
>You'd be my third shoe'?

A long stick of French bread had been drawn in one corner with a beret on its head. It also had legs. And sunglasses. 'L'amour,' said the heart-shaped bubble escaping from the mouth of this loaf.

Those two were the guilty ones, all right.

On the reverse side of the envelope Monty noticed a word he had never seen before. It didn't even look English. SWALK. What did that mean? Was it yet more French? Monty shoved the whole lot between the pages of an atlas.

Overnight the snow came down. The cars on every road took their time that morning. Although the pavements were awash with melting slush, you could still find the makings of a snowball on the tops of walls or

lying on a hedge, and Monty found himself attacked by two people as he approached the school gates. Like most of the girls he knew, those two couldn't throw a snowball to save their lives.

'You missed,' he said.

'Did you get a valentine card this morning?' shouted Anne Clarke, snorting out steam like a dragon.

'No I didn't, hard cheese.'

'Well, we know somebody who sent you one, don't we, Gail?'

'Did you send it?'

'Us?' Anne Clarke released a howl and a giggle into the morning air. 'What makes you think it was *us*?'

Monty did not understand this behaviour, so he went into school hoping that his friend Conor would be back after his dose of the flu.

During the morning he made a point of standing at the back of every line, a tactic which allowed him to go into each classroom last and so avoid Anne Clarke and Gail Summers. If he went in first, they might sit down beside him. Conor couldn't understand why he wasn't pushing and shoving for a radiator seat like everybody else.

In French he put up his hand and asked, quietly, 'Miss Peters, is SWALK a French word?'

She peered at him through the rainbow-framed glasses on the bridge of her nose. She didn't have to peer far, for Monty had been forced to take a seat at the front of the room. Under her nose, in fact.

'What?'

'SWALK, Miss, is it French?'

'Spell it.'

'S-W-A-L-K.'

Some tittering behind made him wonder whether he had asked an intelligent question.

'Are you trying to be funny, Monty Quayle?' said Miss Peters icily, then went on to describe the peculiar habits of some French verb, leaving unsolved the mystery of SWALK.

According to a powerful rumour which invaded the school at lunchtime, all the teachers were afraid of being snowed in and the place was closing early; but that didn't happen. As Conor and Monty walked home at the usual time, Conor – imitating Miss Peters – said, 'Are you trying to be funny, Monty Quayle!' Millions of his flu germs were spluttered over the slushy grey snow. 'I nearly wet myself when you asked her about SWALK.'

And Monty smiled, as if thinking up such humorous things came naturally to him.

'You didn't get a valentine card?' Conor asked shrewdly – a little dart of a question.

'You must be kidding,' said Monty. 'Me? Valentine cards?'

When he got home it was to find that a second card had been delivered to his house, by hand, without a stamp, simply pushed through his front door without so much as a by-your-leave. Monty saw no reason why that sort of thing should be legal.

'Is it from the same person?' his mother wanted to know as she hovered there.

'I don't know,' said Monty, staring at the two words written in capitals on the flap. SWALK and SWALK. Two of them. Plural swalks.

'What does SWALK actually mean?' he asked, making use of his mother.

'Sealed with a loving kiss.'

'Cut out the goo talk, Mum!'

'It does. Goo talk, indeed! S for sealed, W for with, L for loving, K for kiss. It's short for "sealed with a loving kiss".'

Hell's bells! And he'd asked Miss Peters, who now thought of him as a fool, if it was French – she'd think he was girl-mad. Sealed with a loving kiss! Oh, the shame of it, and he hated kissing; his relatives no longer tried it on because he'd put a stop to it – on TV he hated that cissy lip stuff and the horrible sucking noises made by people joined together at their mouths! The humiliation he felt was colossal – his pride all drained away.

He threw the valentine card on the fire and watched until both SWALKs were consumed by it utterly.

'Well, that's not a very nice way to go on,' his mother said. Not that he cared. She had no understanding of the situation whatsoever.

I'll send *them* a card! Monty raved upstairs. I'll send them some card, all right, and it'll be plastered with words the French never heard of. SWAFEJ, he thought. Sealed with a frog's eyeball juice. And SWAMS. Sealed with a monkey's stink. In no time at all he had over a dozen good ones – letters sealed with acid rain, elephant's wee-wee, a pelican's egg yolk, lubricating oil, mashed maggots and worse. Much worse. This line of thinking was effective in its own way, for he had calmed down quite a lot by the time he looked out of his bedroom window and saw both of them standing in the street below.

They had a spaniel-looking dog lolloping round their legs. The sight of this thing's floppy ears and its big soft belly as round as a melon inspired Monty with a cunning idea. Down the stairs he flew three at a time, calling out for Mighty Wolf to appear by his side.

Their yappy mongrel had actually been named Patch for an obvious reason, but he also answered to names like Fleabag, Lagerlout and Mighty Wolf. That dog hated every living thing that did not belong to his own family; and it hated, besides, non-living things within the family. (The hoover was its mortal enemy.) If you held up a mirror he also went berserk, which meant that Mighty Wolf was a creature who even hated himself. Monty opened the front door just enough – and let him loose. Some people were about to learn that it didn't pay to lurk.

This plan backfired horribly, as Monty had to admit when he sneaked down the path some moments later. His fool of a dog was actually showing off in front of the spaniel with a display of athletic twirls and frisky jumps. In between the twirls and jumps there occurred some rubbing of noses. SWALK, thought Monty – bitterly – again. It was as if the creature knew it was St Valentine's Day.

'Your dog likes Sheila,' said Anne Clark.

'He's just friendly,' lied Monty, scooping up the animal into his arms. This was to stop the disgusting smelling of behinds that was now going on.

'Did you get a valentine card?'

'Yes I did.' He was flustered, and could not duck the question.

'We know who sent it even though there's no name on it, don't we, Gail?'

Gail Summers blushed until her cheeks glowed; and then the beast within the cradle of Monty's arms began to whine with desire. A stump of a tail flicked backwards and forwards in front of his face like a windscreen wiper.

'It wants its tea,' Monty explained, retreating smartly up the path and into the house again, where Mighty Wolf got told in no uncertain terms what a big soft wet pudding he had degenerated into.

About the same time on the following day there came a knock at the front door which Monty, to his regret, left for his mother to answer.

She returned saying, 'It's young Gail Summers. She wants to know: is your dog coming out? And you needn't look at me like that – go and speak to her.'

There she stood on his step, with spaniel, wearing a woollen hat and a scarf that seemed to go round her neck at least three times. Not much of her face could be seen, actually.

'Is Patch coming out?' she asked.

Patch, he thought. And how did she get to know Fleabag's real name? No doubt enquiries had been made.

'He's got a thorn in his foot.'

'Is it sore?'

'We had to bathe it.'

'Did you use hot water?'

'And disinfectant,' Monty assured her, while holding on to the door in case Mighty Wolf put in an appearance.

'Well, bye-bye, then,' said Gail, with a twist at Sheila Spaniel's lead, 'I'll see you in school tomorrow.'

'Goodbye,' said Monty, as if he was leaving that night for Australia.

This business about the valentine cards forced him to take a look at himself in the long mirror that evening, and to ask: what could there be about that person on the other side of the looking glass to drive someone to send him a card that was sealed, not once, but twice, with a loving kiss? Surely such magnetism in a human being would be recognizable? All the same, he couldn't find it. After viewing himself from many angles he remained none the wiser.

Going to school next day he noticed Gail Summers on the road ahead of him. Now it was certainly a treacherous morning for walking, and ridges of frozen slush glittered in the early sunlight; but he knew fine rightly that she was not walking slowly because of the ice. The idea was that he should catch up with her, which he did.

'Daddy had to break the ice on our pond this morning,' she said.

'Goldfish?' he said.

'No. It's for wildlife. Goldfish eat tadpoles. One slurp and they're gone.'

'My girlfriend has goldfish,' Monty suddenly blurted out. 'They're big ones as long as your foot, I'd say.'

'Who is she?'

The sheer cheek of this question – the colossal amount of nosiness involved in it – allowed Monty to glare at her angrily.

'It's none of your business who she is.'

'You haven't got one, that's why.'

'That's where you're wrong.'

'Well, who is she, then?'

She didn't believe him! In spite of the fact that he'd even described his girlfriend's goldfish, his word on this important subject was not good enough for her!

'She's Glenda Finch, if you must know.'

Glenda was a rough sort, the sort who pulled hair and who wouldn't take kindly to someone who tried to steal her boyfriend. On the spur of the moment she was a very good choice, Monty was thinking. As he parted company with Gail Summers he felt that he had solved his problem, for anybody with any sense would now find another person to pursue.

At breaktime Conor told him that Glenda Finch was looking for him.

'What for?'

'Dunno,' said Conor. 'Something to do with rumours and goldfish. She says you're saying things about her and she's going to squash you like a grub. You know what she's like.'

Oh God. Only too well, he knew what Glenda was like. No matter which point of the compass she approached from you heard her coming, and you heard her go. She went through life making mountains out of molehills and molehills out of mountains.

Rather like a mole himself, Monty went underground for the rest of the morning. Great care had to be taken while crossing the playground, and he longed for a periscope to enable him to see round corners and down corridors. Often he reflected on the treachery of girls like Gail Summers, who could send you a letter sealed with a loving kiss on a Tuesday and then land you right in it the day after.

At lunchtime Glenda Finch trapped him in the crowded room where people went to eat their sandwiches. There was, in fact, an open window to hand, but only a genuine coward could have done a bunk like that.

'You're saying things about me, Monty Quayle! You said I'm your *girlfriend*!'

The whole situation – he saw as one detached – was just completely crazy. And the craziest thing of all was that, yes, somehow he *had* said that. My girlfriend is Glenda Finch, he'd said. And why? He must have been temporarily insane. Glenda could never be anyone's girlfriend, for crying out loud, it would be too dangerous.

'And you said I sent you a valentine card! You'd better watch it, Quayle. I wouldn't send you a valentine card for a pension and I wouldn't be your girlfriend if you were the last person left alive after a nuclear bomb. And I haven't got *goldfish*!' she screamed, finishing on a high note. Monty wondered desperately if he could pretend that there was another Glenda Finch.

There was more. Monty fought back with such statements as 'Shut your spout, fat whale,' in order to avoid being overwhelmed completely. After the contest he felt quite tingly and invigorated – as joggers must do, he reflected.

And Gail Summers did not trouble him from that time on.

The days raced by, and the long evenings of summer came again. That was the year when the Quayle family went abroad for the first time on a camping holiday in Northern France. Part of the thinking behind the holiday was that Monty would get a chance to practise his French, but he spent the time playing with English-speaking children and got by with a few French words for sweets. While they were away Mighty Wolf attacked a moving Volkswagen in the street and banjoed his leg. The mutt recovered all right, but once arthritis set into his left hip he could hardly muster the enthusiasm to see off a stray cat.

Two more summers went by. Monty found himself looking up at the sky at night, and wondered about the distances between the stars – a thing he had never done before. It made him sense for the first time the possible insignificance of terrestrial affairs. On some occasions he experienced in the evenings what he himself described as 'the coloured peace of sunsets'; on others, he felt disturbed by vague longings which he could not name. He grew conscious of his appearance and cared especially for his hair. The thought of going thin on top like his dad scared the wits out of him.

The girl he fancied was Gail Summers. Wherever he went he carried in his mind's eye the fling of her dark hair and the swaying of her body – these were things he could not forget, and to hear her laughing in the company of other people was like hearing laughter over the wall of a scented garden from which a time warp had excluded him. In his heart – figuratively speaking, of course – he conceded that if he had three feet she'd be his third shoe: but she was now going strong with some fellow from Bell's Hill.

Uninvited Ghosts
Penelope Lively

Marian and Simon were sent to bed early on the day that the Brown family moved house. By then everyone had lost their temper with everyone else; the cat had been sick on the sitting-room carpet; the dog had run away twice. If you have ever moved you will know what kind of a day it had been. Packing cases and newspaper all over the place . . . sandwiches instead of proper meals . . . the kettle lost and a wardrobe stuck on the stairs and Mrs Brown's favourite vase broken. There was bread and baked beans for supper, the television wouldn't work and the water wasn't hot so when all was said and done the children didn't object too violently to being packed off to bed. They'd had enough, too. They had one last argument about who was going to sleep by the window, put on their pyjamas, got into bed, switched the lights out . . . and it was at that point that the ghost came out of the bottom drawer of the chest of drawers.

It oozed out, a grey cloudy shape about three feet long, smelling faintly of wood-smoke, sat down on a chair and began to hum to itself. It looked like a bundle of bedclothes, except that it was not solid: you could see, quite clearly, the cushion on the chair beneath it.

Marian gave a shriek. 'That's a ghost!'

'Oh, be quiet, dear, do,' said the ghost. 'That noise goes right through my head. And it's not nice to call people names.' It look out a ball of wool and some needles and began to knit.

What would you have done? Well, yes – Simon and Marian did just that and I dare say you can imagine what happened. You try telling your mother that you can't get

to sleep because there's a ghost sitting in the room
clacking its knitting-needles and humming. Mrs Brown
said the kind of things she could be expected to say and
the ghost continued sitting there knitting and humming
and Mrs Brown went out, banging the door and saying
threatening things about if there's so much as another
word from either of you . . .

'She can't see it,' said Marian to Simon.

''Course not, dear,' said the ghost. 'It's the kiddies I'm
here for. Love kiddies, I do. We're going to be ever such
friends.'

'Go away!' yelled Simon. 'This is our house now!'

'No it isn't,' said the ghost smugly. 'Always been here,
I have. A hundred years and more. Seen plenty of
families come and go, I have. Go to bye-byes now, there's
good children.'

The children glared at it and buried themselves under
the bedclothes. And, eventually, slept.

The next night it was there again. This time it was
smoking a long white pipe and reading a newspaper
dated 1842. Beside it was a second grey cloudy shape.
'Hello, dearies,' said the ghost. 'Say how do you do to my
Auntie Edna.'

'She can't come here too,' wailed Marian.

'Oh yes she can,' said the ghost. 'Always comes here in
August, does Auntie. She likes a change.'

Auntie Edna was even worse, if possible. She sucked
peppermint drops that smelled so strong that Mrs
Brown, when she came to kiss the children goodnight,
looked suspiciously under their pillows. She also sang
hymns in a loud squeaky voice. The children lay there
groaning and the ghosts sang and rustled the news-
papers and ate peppermints.

The next night there were three of them. 'Meet Uncle
Charlie!' said the first ghost. The children groaned.

'And Jip,' said the ghost. 'Here, Jip, good dog – come and say hello to the kiddies, then.' A large grey dog that you could see straight through came out from under the bed, wagging its tail. The cat, who had been curled up beside Marian's feet (it was supposed to sleep in the kitchen, but there are always ways for a resourceful cat to get what it wants), gave a howl and shot on top of the wardrobe, where it sat spitting. The dog lay down in the middle of the rug and set about scratching itself vigorously; evidently it had ghost fleas, too.

Uncle Charlie was unbearable. He had a loud cough that kept going off like a machine-gun and he told the longest most pointless stories the children had ever heard. He said he too loved kiddies and he knew kiddies loved stories. In the middle of the seventh story the children went to sleep out of sheer boredom.

The following week the ghosts left the bedroom and were to be found all over the house. The children had no peace at all. They'd be quietly doing their homework and all of a sudden Auntie Edna would be breathing down their necks reciting arithmetic tables. The original ghost took to sitting on top of the television with his legs in front of the picture. Uncle Charlie told his stories all through the best programmes and the dog lay permanently at the top of the stairs. The Browns' cat became quite hysterical, refused to eat and went to live on the top shelf of the kitchen dresser.

Something had to be done. Marian and Simon also were beginning to show the effects; their mother decided they looked peaky and bought an appalling sticky brown vitamin medicine from the chemists to strengthen them. 'It's the ghosts!' wailed the children. 'We don't need vitamins!' Their mother said severely that she didn't want to hear another word of this silly nonsense about ghosts. Auntie Edna, who was sitting smirking on the other side of the kitchen table at that very moment, nodded vigorously and took out a packet of humbugs which she sucked noisily.

'We've got to get them to go and live somewhere else,' said Marian. But where, that was the problem, and how? It was then that they had a bright idea. On Sunday the Browns were all going to see their uncle who was rather rich and lived alone in a big house with thick carpets everywhere and empty rooms and the biggest colour television you ever saw. Plenty of room for ghosts.

They were very cunning. They suggested to the ghosts that they might like a drive in the country. The ghosts said at first that they were quite comfortable where they were, thank you, and they didn't fancy these new-fangled motor cars, not at their time of life. But then Auntie Edna remembered that she liked looking at the pretty flowers and the trees and finally they agreed to give it a try. They sat in a row on the back shelf of the car. Mrs Brown kept asking why there was such a strong smell of peppermint and Mr Brown kept roaring at Simon and Marian to keep still while he was driving. The fact was that the ghosts were shoving them; it was like being nudged by three cold damp flannels. And the ghost dog, who had come along too of course, was carsick.

When they got to Uncle Dick's the ghosts came in and had a look round. They liked the expensive carpets and the enormous television. They slid in and out of the wardrobes and walked through the doors and the walls and sent Uncle Dick's budgerigars into a decline from which they have never recovered. Nice place, they said, nice and comfy.

'Why not stay here?' said Simon, in an offhand tone.

'Couldn't do that,' said the ghosts firmly. 'No kiddies. Dull. We like a place with a bit of life to it.' And they piled back into the car and sang hymns all the way home to the

Browns' house. They also ate toast. There were real toast-crumbs on the floor and the children got the blame.

Simon and Marian were in despair. The ruder they were to the ghosts the more the ghosts liked it. 'Cheeky!' they said indulgently. 'What a cheeky little pair of kiddies! There now . . . come and give uncle a kiss.' The children weren't even safe in the bath. One or other of the ghosts could come and sit on the taps and talk to them. Uncle Charlie had produced a mouth-organ and played the same tune over and over again; it was quite excruciating. The children went around with their hands over their ears. Mrs Brown took them to the doctor to find out if there was something wrong with their hearing. The children knew better than to say anything to the doctor about the ghosts. It was pointless saying anything to anyone.

I don't know what would have happened if Mrs Brown hadn't happened to make friends with Mrs Walker from down the road. Mrs Walker had twin babies, and one day she brought the babies along for tea.

Now one baby is bad enough. Two babies are trouble in a big way. These babies created pandemonium. When they weren't both howling they were crawling around the floor pulling the table-cloths off the tables or hitting their heads on the chairs and hauling the books out of the bookcases. They threw their food all over the kitchen and flung cups of milk on the floor. Their mother mopped up after them and every time she tried to have a conversation with Mrs Brown the babies bawled in chorus so that no one could hear a word.

In the middle of this the ghosts appeared. One baby was yelling its head off and the other was gluing pieces of chewed-up bread on to the front of the television. The ghosts swooped down on them with happy cries. 'Oh!' they trilled. 'Bless their little hearts then, diddums, give auntie a smile then.' And the babies stopped in mid-howl and gazed at the ghosts. The ghosts cooed at the babies and the babies cooed at the ghosts. The ghosts chattered to the babies and sang them songs and the babies chattered back and were as good as gold for the next hour and their mother had the first proper conversation she'd had in weeks. When they went the ghosts stood in a row at the window, waving.

Simon and Marian knew when to seize an opportunity. That evening they had a talk with the ghosts. At first the ghosts raised objections. They didn't fancy the idea of moving, they said; you got set in your ways, at their age; Auntie Edna reckoned a strange house would be the death of her.

The children talked about the babies, relentlessly.

And the next day they led the ghosts down the road, followed by the ghost dog, and into the Walkers' house. Mrs Walker doesn't know to this day why the babies, who had been screaming for the last half hour, suddenly stopped and broke into great smiles. And she has never understood why, from that day forth, the babies became the most tranquil, quiet, amiable babies in the area. The ghosts kept the babies amused from morning to night. The babies thrived; the ghosts were happy; the ghost dog, who was actually a bitch, settled down so well that she had puppies which is one of the most surprising aspects of the whole business. The Brown children heaved a sigh of relief and got back to normal life. The babies, though, I have to tell you, grew up somewhat peculiar.

The Harry Hastings Method
Warner Law

Susie Plimson says I should keep on practising my writing. She's been my teacher at Hollywood High Adult Education in the professional writing course and says I am still having trouble with my syntaxes and my tenses, and very kindly gave me private lessons at her place, and she is dark-haired and very pretty and about my age (which is twenty-five).

Susie says if I really want to be a professional writer, I should write about what I really know about – if it is interesting – and while I did do a spell in the navy some time back, I was on a destroyer tender and never heard a shot fired except in practice, which I don't think is a highly interesting matter to describe.

But one thing I know a lot about is working the houses in the Hollywood hills. The people who live up there are not particularly stinking rich, but then, I've never been interested in valuable paintings or diamond necklaces, anyway, because what do you do with them?

But there are usually portable radios and TV sets and tape decks and now and then there is some cash lying around, or a fur, or a few pieces of fairly good jewellery, or maybe a new leather jacket – all things easy to dispose of.

This is an area of winding streets and a lot of trees and bushes, and the houses are mostly set back from the street and are some distance from their neighbours, and so it is an easy vicinity to work.

There's no bus service up there at all, so everybody needs a car or two, and if there is no auto in the carport, you can be pretty sure that no one is home.

There are rural-type mailboxes on the street, and people are always stuffing them with business cards and circulars, like ads for house cleaning and landscaping and such.

So I had a lot of cards printed for various things, like for a house-painting firm, and some for the 'Bulldog Burglar Protection Agency', which says we will install all kinds of silent burglar alarms, and bells will ring in our office and we will have radio cars there in a few minutes.

I also have some Pest Control and House Repair cards. None of these firms exists, of course, but neither do the phone numbers on my cards.

But while I drive slowly around the hills in my little VW bus and put my cards in the boxes, I can get a pretty good idea of who is home and who isn't, and who is gone all day, and so forth.

By the way, my truck is lettered with: H. STRUSSMAN INC, GENERAL HOUSE REPAIRS on one side and FERGUSON PEST CONTROL, EVERYBODY LOVES US BUT YOUR PESTS! on the other side.

I make these up myself. My theory is that nobody can ever see both sides of my truck at the same time, which will really confuse witnesses, if there are any. Of course I change the truck signs every week, and every month I paint the truck a different colour.

When I decide that a certain house is ripe for hitting, I go up and ring the doorbell. If I am wrong and someone is home – this is seldom – I ask them if their house happens to be swarming with disease-infested rats. Since there are no rats at all in these hills, they always say no and I leave.

If nobody answers the doorbell, it is, of course, another matter. Most of these houses have locks that could be opened by blindfolded monkeys. Not one of them has any kind of burglar alarm.

There are watchdogs in some houses, but these I avoid, because you never know a friendly dog from a vicious one until you've been chewed up. And, of course, I would not hurt any dog if you paid me.

What I am getting to is about one particular house up there. It's a fairly new one-storey modern style, up a driveway, but you can see the carport from the street below. In casing the place for some time, I figured that a man probably lived there alone.

There was only one car, a great big new Mercedes, and this man drove off every weekday morning at nine. I saw him a few times and he was a nice-looking gentleman of about forty-five. He was always gone all day, so I guessed he had an office job.

So one day, I drove my truck up the driveway and got out and saw a sign: BEWARE OF THE DOG – and, at the same time, this little pooch comes out of a dog door and up to me, and he is a black bundle of hair and the wiggliest, happiest little puppy you ever saw.

I picked him up and let him lick my face and saw that he had a tag on his collar that read: CUDDLES, MY OWNER IS HARRY HASTINGS. There was also a phone number.

I rang the doorbell, but nobody came. The front-door lock was so stupid that I opened it with a plastic card.

Inside – well, you have never seen such a sloppy-kept house. Not dirty – just sloppy. There was five days' worth of dishes in the sink.

I found out later that this Harry Hastings has a maid who comes and cleans once a week, but meantime, this character just throws his dirty shirts and socks on the floor. What a slob.

I turned out to be right about his living alone. There was only one single bed in use – which, of course, was not made, and I doubt if he makes it from one year to the

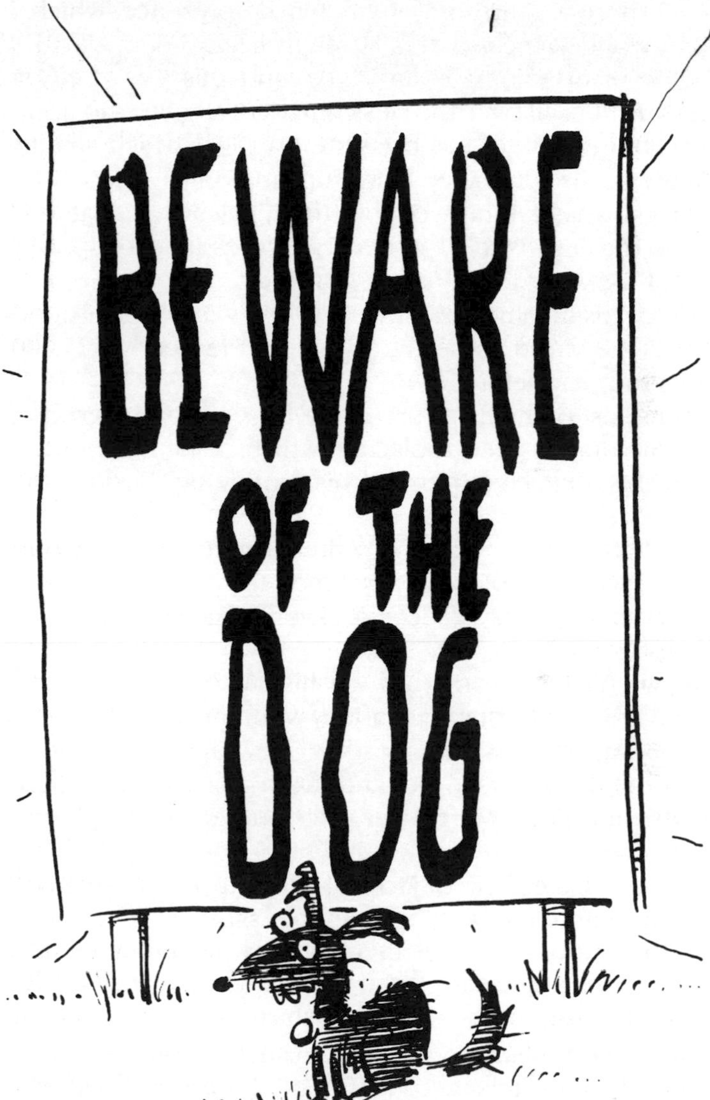
BEWARE
OF THE
DOG

next. There was no sign of any female presence, which I don't wonder, the way this Hastings lives.

One of his rooms is an office, and this was *really* a mess. Papers all over the desk and also all over the floor. This room stank of old cigarette butts, of which smell I am very conscious since I gave up smoking.

From what I found on his desk, I learned that this Harry Hastings is a TV writer. He writes kind of spooky stuff. I took one of his scripts, to study.

From his income-tax returns, which were lying around for all the world to see, I saw he made nearly $23,000 gross the year before.

But most of the furniture in the house is pretty grubby, and the drapes need replacing, which made me wonder what this character spent all his money on, besides the Mercedes.

He had a new electric typewriter and a great big colour-TV set, which would take four men to move, and a hi-fi, but no art objects or decent silver or gold cufflinks or things like that.

It wasn't till I went through his clothes closet that I found out that most of his money went into his wardrobe. There was about $5000 worth of new apparel in there, most of it hand-tailored and from places like where Sinatra and Dean Martin get their outfits. Very flash and up-to-date.

I tried on a couple of jackets, and it turns out that this Hastings and me are exactly the same size! I mean exactly. These clothes looked like they had been tailored for me alone, after six fittings. Only his shoes didn't fit me, sad to say.

I was very pleased, indeed, I can tell you, as I have always had trouble getting fitted off the rack. Also, I like to dress in the latest fashion when I take Susie to nice places.

So I took the entire wardrobe, including shirts and ties. I decided to take the typewriter, which I needed for my writing-class homework. The machine I had kept skipping.

But I wanted to try out the typewriter before I took it, and also, I thought I would leave a note for this Hastings, so he wouldn't think I was some kind of crude thug. So I typed:

Dear Mr Hastings,

I am typing this to see if your typewriter works OK. I see that it does. I am not taking it to sell but I need it because I am trying to become a professional writer like you, which I know because I saw your scripts on your desk, and I am taking one to help me with my work, for studying.

I wish to to make you a compliment anent your fine wardrobe of clothes. As it happened, they are like they have been made for me only. I am not taking them to sell them but because I need some good clothes to wear. Your shoes do not fit me, so I am leaving them.

I am also not taking your hi-fi, because there is a terrible screech in the treble. I like your dog, and I will give him a biskit.

A Friend

Well, some three months or so now passed, because there was no sense in hitting Hastings' house again until he had time to get a new bunch of clothes together.

But when I thought the time was ripe, I drove by there again and saw a little VW in the carport, and also, there was a big blonde woman shaking rugs.

I drove up and asked her if her house was swarming with disease-infested rats and she said she didn't think so but that she was only the once-a-week cleaning lady. She sounded Scandinavian. I took note that this was a Wednesday.

I went back the next Monday. No car in the carport. But on the way to the house, there was a new sign, hand-lettered on a board, and it read: BEWARE! VICIOUS WATCHDOG ON DUTY! THIS DOG HAS BEEN TRAINED TO ATTACK AND MEAN IT! YOU HAVE BEEN WARNED! PROCEED NO FARTHER!

Well, this gives me pause, as you can well imagine. But then I remember that this Hastings is a writer with an ingenious and inventive mind, and I do not believe this sign for one moment. Cuddles is my friend.

So I start for the house, and suddenly, this enormous alsatian jumps through the dog door and runs straight at me, growling and snarling, and then he leaps and knocks me down, and sure enough, starts chewing me to pieces.

But then out comes Cuddles, and I am sure there is a dog language, for he woofed at this monster dog as if in reproach, as if to say: 'Knock it off. This is a friend. Leave him alone.' So pretty soon, both dogs are licking me.

But when I get to the front door, I find that this Hastings has installed a new, burglar-proof lock. I walk around the house and find that there are new locks on both the kitchen door and the laundry-room door. They must have set Hastings back about seventy-five bucks.

There are also a lot of sliding-glass doors around the house, but I don't like to break plate glass, because I know how expensive it is to replace.

But I finally locate a little louvred window by the laundry-room door, and I find that by breaking only one louvre and cutting the screen, I can reach through and around and open the door.

Inside, I find that the house is just as messy as before. This guy will *die* a slob.

But when I get to his bedroom, here is this note, taped to his closet door. It is dusty and looks like it has been there for months. It says:

> Dear Burglar,
>
> Just in *case* you are the same young man who was in here a few months ago, I think I must tell you that you have a long way to go before you will be a professional writer.
>
> 'Anent' is archaic and should be avoided. A 'wardrobe of clothes' is redundant. It is 'biscuit', not 'biskit'. Use your dictionary!
>
> I know you are a young man, because both my cleaning woman and a nineteen-year-old neighbour have seen you and your truck. If you have gotten this far into my house, you cannot be stupid. Have you ever thought of devoting your talents to something a little higher than burgling people such as me?
>
> Harry Hastings

Inside his closet are two fabulous new suits, plus a really great red-and-blue plaid cashmere sports coat. I take these and am about to leave when I remember there is something I want to tell Hastings.

In his office, there is a new electric typewriter, on which I type:

> Dear Mr Hastings,
>
> Thank you for your help. In return, I want to tell you that I read the script of yours I took and I think it is pretty good, except that I don't believe that the man should go back to his wife. I mean, after she

tried to poison him three times. This is just my opinion, of course.

I do not have a dictionary, so I am taking yours. Thank you.

A Friend

I, of course, do not take his new typewriter, partly because I already have one and also because I figure he will need it to make money with so he can replace his wardrobe again.

Four months go by before I figure it is time to hit the house again. By this time, my clothes are getting kind of tired, and also the styles have changed some.

This time, when I drive up to the house one afternoon, there is a new hand-lettered sign: THIS HOUSE IS PROTECTED BY THE BULLDOG BURGLAR PROTECTION AGENCY! THERE ARE SILENT ALARMS EVERYWHERE! IF THEY ARE TRIPPED, RADIO CARS WILL CONVERGE AT ONCE! PROCEED NO FARTHER! YOU HAVE BEEN WARNED!

Come on now! I and I alone am the *nonexistent* Bulldog Burglar Protection Agency! I'd put my card in his mailbox! This is really one cheap stinker, this Harry Hastings.

When I get near the house, the dogs come out, and I give them a little loving, and then I see a note on the front door.

Dear Jack,

Welcome! Hope you had a nice trip. The key is hidden where it always has been. I didn't have to go to work today. I've run down the hill to get some scotch and some steaks. Be back in a few minutes. The gals are coming at six.

Harry

Well, this gives me pause. I finally decide that this is not the right day to hit the house. This could, of course, be another of Hastings' tricks, but I can't be sure. So I leave.

But a few days later, I come back and this same note to Jack is still on the door, only now it is all yellowed. You would think that this lame-brain would at least write a new note every day, welcoming Bert or Sam or Harriet or Hazel or whoever.

The truth is that this Hastings is so damn smart, when you think about it, that he is actually stupid.

The broken louvre and the screen have by now been replaced, but when I break the glass and cut the screen and reach around to open the laundry door, I find that he has installed chains and bolts on the inside.

Well, as any idiot knows, you can't bolt all your doors from the inside when you go out, so one door has to be openable, and I figure it has to be the front door; but the only way I can get in is to break a big frosted-plate-glass window to the left of it and reach through and open the door.

As I said, I'm not happy to break plate glass, but this Hastings has left me no choice, so I knock out a hole just big enough for me to reach through and open the door and go in.

This time, there is *another* note on his closet door.

Dear Burglar,

Are you incapable of pity? By how, you must be the best-dressed burglar in Hollywood. But how many clothes can you *wear*? You might like to know that my burglary insurance has been cancelled. My new watchdog cost me one hundred dollars and I have spent a small fortune on new locks and bolts and chains.

Now I fear you are going to start smashing my plate-glass windows, which can cost as much as ninety dollars to replace. There is only one new suit in this closet! All my other clothes I keep now either in my car or at my office. Take the suit, if you must, but never return, or you will be sorry, indeed, if you do. I have a terrible revenge in mind.

Harry Hastings

P.S. You still have time to reform yourself.

P.P.S. I don't like his going back to his poisoning wife, either. But the network insisted on a 'Happy Ending'.

H.H.

Well, I am not about to fall for all this noise about pity. Any man who has a dog trained to go for me and who uses my own Bulldog Agency against me is not, in my mind, deserving of too much sympathy.

So I take the suit, which is a just beautiful Edwardian eight-button, in grey shark-skin.

Now, quite a few months pass and I begin to feel a little sorry for this character, and I decide to let him alone, forever.

But then, one day, when I am out working, some louse breaks into my own pad, which is three rooms over a private garage in Hollywood. He takes every stitch of clothing I own.

By this time, I am heavily dating Susie Plimson, and she likes good dressers. So, while I am not too happy about it, I decide I have to pay Hastings another visit.

No dogs come out this time when I walk to the front door. But on it is a typed note, which says:

HELGA! DO NOT OPEN THIS DOOR! Since you were here last week, I bought a PUMA for burglar protection. This is a huge cat, a cougar or a mountain lion, about four feet long, not including the tail. The man I bought it from told me it was fairly tame, but it is NOT!

It has tried to attack both dogs, who are OK and are locked in the guest room. I myself have just gone down to my doctor's to have stitches taken in my face and neck and arms. The ferocious puma is wandering loose inside the house.

The SPCA people are coming soon to capture it and take it away. I tried to call you and tell you not to come today, but you had already left. Whatever you do, if the SPCA has not come before you, DO NOT UNDER ANY CIRCUMSTANCES OPEN THIS DOOR!!

Well, naturally, this gave me considerable pause. Helga was obviously the blonde cleaning woman. But this was a Tuesday, and she came on Wednesdays. Or she used to. But she could have changed her days.

I stroll around the outside of the house. But all of the curtains and drapes are drawn, and I can't see in. As I pass the guest-room windows, the two dogs bark inside. So this much of the note on the door is true.

So I wander back to the front door, and I think and I ponder. Is there really a puma in there, or is this just another of Hastings' big fat dirty lies?

After all, it is one hell of a lot of trouble to buy and keep a puma just to protect a few clothes. And it is also expensive, and this Hastings I know by now is a cheapskate.

It costs him not one thin dime to put this stupid note to Helga on his front door and, God knows, it would terrify most anybody who wanted to walk in.

Susie told us in class that in every story, there is like a moment of decision. I figured this was mine.

After about five minutes of solid thought, I finally make my decision. There *is* no puma in there. It's just that Hastings wants me to think that there is a puma in there.

So I decide to enter the house, by breaking another hole in the now replaced frosted-plate-glass window to the left of the front door. So I break out a small portion of this glass.

And I peer through this little hole I've made, and I see nothing. No puma. I listen. I don't hear any snarling cat or anything. No puma. Just the same, there *could* be a puma in there and it could be crouching silently just inside the door, waiting to pounce and bite my hand off when I put it in.

Very carefully, I put some fingers in and wiggle them. No puma. And so I put my arm in and reach and turn the doorknob from the inside and open the door a crack.

No snarl from a puma – whatever pumas snarl like. I open the door a little wider and I call, 'Here, pussy-pussy! Here, puma-puma! *Nice* puma!' No response.

I creep in very cautiously, looking around, ready to jump back and out and slam the door on this beast, if necessary. But there is no puma.

And then I realize that my decision was, of course, right, and there is no lousy puma in this damn house. But still, I am sweating like a pig and breathing heavily, and I suddenly figure out what Susie means when she talks about 'the power of the written word'.

With just a piece of writing, this Hastings transferred an idea from his crazy imagination into my mind, and I was willing to believe it.

So I walk down the hall to his bedroom door, which is shut, and there is *another* typed note on it:

Dear Burglar,
    OK, so there is no puma. Did you really think I'd let a huge cat mess up my nice neat house?

However, I am going to give you a *serious warning*. DO NOT OPEN THIS DOOR! One of the engineers at our studio has invented a highly sophisticated security device and I've borrowed one of his models.

It's hidden in the bedroom and it works by means of ultrasonic waves. They are soundless and they have a fantastically destructive and permanent effect on brain tissues. It takes less than a minute of exposure.

You will not notice any brain-numbing effects at once, but in a few days, your memory will start to go, and then your reasoning powers, and so, for your *own* sake DO NOT ENTER THIS ROOM!

Harry Hastings

Well, I really had to hand it to this loony character. No wonder he made a lot of money as a writer. I, of course, do not believe *one word* of this, *at all*; therefore, I go into the bedroom and hurry to see if there is any hidden electronic device but, of course, there is not. Naturally.

Then I see another note, on the closet door, and it says:

Dear Burglar,

I don't suppose I should have expected you to believe that one, with your limited imagination and your one-track mind. By the way, where do you go in all my clothes? You must be quite a swinger.

There are only a few new things in the closet. But before you take them, I suggest you sniff them. You will notice a kind of cologne smell, but this is only to disguise another *odour*. I have a pal who was in chemical warfare, and he has given me a liquid that can be sprayed inside clothing. No amount of dry cleaning can ever entirely remove it.

When the clothes are worn, the heat of the body converts this substance into a heavy gas that attacks the skin and produces the most frightful and agonisingly painful blisters, from the ankles to the neck. Never forget that you have been *warned*.

Harry Hastings

Well, I don't believe this for one moment, and so I open the closet door. All there is is one pair of slacks and a sports coat. But this coat looks like the very same *plaid cashmere* I took before and the rat stole from *me*!

But then I realize this could not be so, but it was just that Hastings liked this coat so much he went out and bought another just like it.

Anyway, I find myself sniffing these. They smell of cologne, all right, but nothing else, and I know, of course, that this kind of gas stuff does not exist at all except in Hastings' wild imagination, which I am coming to admire by now.

As I drive back to my pad, I start to laugh when I think of all the stupid and fantastic things that Hastings has tried to put into my mind today by the power of suggestion, and I realize that he almost succeeded. *Almost*, but not quite.

When I get home and climb the outside stairs to my front door, there are *three envelopes* taped to it, one above another. There are no names on them, but they are numbered, 1, 2, 3. I do not know what in hell all this could be about, but I open 1 and read:

Dear Burglar,

The plaid cashmere coat you have over your arm right now is *not* a replacement for the one you stole.

It is the *same identical coat*. Think about this before you open envelope 2.

Harry Hastings

Well, of *course*, I think about this as I stand there with my mouth sort of hanging open. All of a sudden, it *hits* me! *Harry Hastings* was the rat who stole all his clothes back! But how did he know where I *live*? How could he know I was going to hit his house *today*? My hands are all fumbles as I open 2. Inside it says:

Dear Burglar,

To answer your questions: On your *third* visit to my house, my young neighbour saw you and followed you home in his car, and so found out just where you live. Later, in my own good time, I easily entered this place with a bent paper clip and retrieved my own clothes. Today, my neighbour called me at my office and said you were inside my house again.

Later, I phoned him and he said you had come out, with my coat. So I've had time to come here and write and leave these notes. I also have had time to do something else, which you will read about in 3.

Harry Hastings

I open this third envelope very fast indeed, because I figure that if Hastings knows all this, the fuzz will be along any minute. In it I read:

Dear Burglar,

I got the puma idea from a friend out in the valley who has one in a large cage in his yard. Long ago, I asked him if I might borrow this huge cat for a day sometime, and he said yes and that he didn't like burglars, either. He has a large carrying cage for the puma. I called him this morning the moment I heard you were inside my house, and he drove the puma right *over here*, and we released the huge cat inside your place. She is now in there, wandering around loose.

I have done this partly because I am vengeful and vindictive by nature and partly because I've made my living for years as a verisimilitudinous (look it up later) writer, and I deeply resent anyone I cannot fool. The puma that is now inside is my childish way of getting even.

This is no *trick* this time! If you have any brains at *all*, DO NOT OPEN THIS DOOR! Just get out of town before the police arrive, which will be in about half an hour. Goodbye.

Harry Hastings

P.S. The puma's name is Carrie – as if that would help you any.

Well, I read in a story once where somebody was called a 'quivering mass of indecisive jelly', and that is what I was right then. I simply did not know *what* to think or believe. If this was any door but mine, I could walk away. But all my *cash* was hidden inside, and I *had* to get it before I could leave town.

So I stand there and I sweat and I think and I think and after a long time, it comes to me that *this* time, Hastings is finally telling the *truth*. Besides I can hear little noises from inside. There *is* a puma in there! I know it! But I have to get in there, just the same!

I finally figure that if I open the door fast and step back, Carrie might just scoot past me and away. But maybe she will attack me.

But then I figure if I wrap the sports coat around one arm and the slacks around the other, maybe I can fend off

Carrie long enough to grab a chair and then force her into my bathroom, the way lion tamers do, and then slam the door on her, and then grab my cash and run out of there, and the police can worry about her when they come.

So this is what I decide to do, only it is some time before I can get up the nerve to unlock the door and push it open. I unlock the door and I stand there. But finally, I think, 'Oh, hell, you *got* to do it, sooner or later,' and so I push my door open and stand back.

No puma jumps at me. Nothing happens at all. But then I look around the corner of my door and *Harry Hastings* is sitting inside. Not with a gun or anything. He is sitting very calmly behind the old card table I use as a desk, with a cigarette in his mouth and a pencil in his hand, and I see one of my stories in front of him.

I walk in and just stand there with my face on and cannot think of any clever remark to make, when he says: 'Tell me one thing. *Did* you or did you *not* really believe there was a puma in here?'

If I remember right – I was pretty shook up then – I nodded and I said, 'Yes, sir. Yes. I really did.'

Then he smiled a big smile and said, 'Well, thank heavens for *that*, I was beginning to think I was losing my grip. I feel a little better now. Sit down. I want to talk to you. By the way, your syntax is terrible and your grammar is worse. I've been making some corrections while waiting for you. However, that's not what I want to talk to you about. Sit down. Stop trembling, will you, and sit down!'

I sat.

As I write now, I am the co-owner and manager of the Puma Burglar Protection Agency. Harry Hastings is my silent partner and he put up two thousand dollars for financing. Susie helps me with my accounts. I have 130 clients now, at five dollars a month each.

The reason it's so cheap is that we use the Harry Hastings Method. That is, we don't bother with burglar alarms or things like that, I just patrol around and keep putting up and changing signs and notices and notes on front doors. Already, the burglary rate in my area has been cut by two-thirds.

This very morning, I got a little letter from Harry Hastings with two new ideas for front-door notes. One is: CLARA! I HAVE ALREADY CALLED THE POLICE AND THEY WILL BE HERE IN MINUTES! DO NOT CALL THEM AGAIN! GEORGE IS LOCKED IN THE BATHROOM AND CAN'T GET OUT, SO WE WILL BE SAFE TILL THEY GET HERE!

The second one is: NOTICE! BECAUSE OF A FRIGHTFULLY CONTAGIOUS DISEASE, THIS HOUSE HAS BEEN EVACUATED AND QUARANTINED. IT MUST ABSOLUTELY NOT BE ENTERED UNTIL IT HAS BEEN FUMIGATED!

Harry Hastings says that I should be sure to warn the householder to remove this notice before any large parties.

A Ghost of One's Own
Ursula Moray Williams

Harriet was in the bus, on her way to a party, carrying her family ghost in a basket. She was going to see Miss Meadie, who was giving the party at her home. Her brother William sat on the seat opposite to her, looking sulky, because he had not wanted to come.

Some people can see ghosts and some cannot. Harriet, alone of all her family, could. Her brother William could not, but he could feel them and hear them. And he could smell them, for some ghosts have a fragrance very like old herbs and roses. William did not care for ghosts, so this caused him a lot of inconvenience.

The rest of the family just did not believe in them at all. So they would not be likely to take any notice of the advertisement in a column of the local paper that said: 'All Ghosts Welcome at Miss Meadie's Party on Friday Next.' It did not say who Miss Meadie was, nor where she lived, but anyone who really wanted to go to the party could surely find out.

Harriet had found out long ago, before she had a ghost of her own, when she was riding her bicycle back from school and had turned aside to explore the driveway of an old country estate. Harriet recognized it at once as ghost territory, even before she met Miss Meadie coming down the drive carrying armfuls of freshly cut phantom roses which could not possibly be real, since it was February. There was a ghost dog at her heels, and a real one, and two semi-invisible cats, also an old butler, who looked at Harriet and vanished.

Miss Meadie recognized Harriet at once as a Ghost Believer. She gave her a rose and invited her to tea.

'You must come and visit me whenever you like!' Miss Meadie told her. 'And bring your friends with you. I mean your personal friends of course, not your flesh-and-blood ones. I know just what it is like to have your dear ones snubbed and slighted and ignored and not believed in. You must bring them to me instead!'

Harriet was too embarrassed to explain that she had no phantom of her own at present. True, she saw and heard other people's wherever she went, but they all belonged to someone else.

'You do have a ghost of your own, I suppose?' Miss Meadie said sharply, and for a moment Harriet felt that she had arrived under false pretences.

She saved herself by saying calmly: 'Well, just at present I haven't got one, but my brother William has a skeleton.'

'A skeleton?' said Miss Meadie with interest. 'And why has he not come to see me?'

'My brother,' Harriet explained, 'doesn't like ghosts!'

'Doesn't *like* them?' Miss Meadie repeated. 'But they are lovely things! So gentle! So affectionate . . . so beautiful! Why doesn't your brother William think that ghosts are beautiful?'

'My brother can't *see* ghosts,' Harriet explained. 'He can only hear and feel them. It makes it difficult for him. But he found the skeleton in the loft, himself, and although he can't see it he seems very fond of it. It goes everywhere with him, except to school. It is a very quiet skeleton, only sometimes it has some mischievous ways. It trips up my father in the hall when William leaves it around. My father does not believe in ghosts at all.'

'So sad!' said Miss Meadie. 'So sad!'

'I must be going now,' said Harriet.

'Very well,' said Miss Meadie. 'Come back when you have a ghost of your own.'

Harriet felt that she had fallen short of Miss Meadie's expectations. The parting was a little cold. But she had no idea where she could get a ghost for herself. You couldn't buy them, and William's had arrived quite by accident, due to rummaging in the loft on a wet day in the holidays. As far as Harriet was concerned, he was welcome to it. She did not care for skeletons, but since meeting Miss Meadie she had realized that just seeing ghosts was not enough for a true ghost lover. One ought to have a phantom of one's own.

She did, quite soon.

Harriet and William lived in one half of a semi-detached Victorian villa. The baby belonging to the people in the other half cried all night long, but when their mother mentioned it to the baby's mother she was most indignant, and said that the baby slept in her room and never woke up all night, ever.

'I didn't hear it myself. It was the children who mentioned it.' Harriet's mother said, apologizing hastily.

The next time the baby cried, Harriet took a torch, woke her brother William, and climbed the stairs to the loft. There was a thin partition between their part of the loft and the next-door part. The baby was crying on the other side. Harriet made a hole in the partition, clambered through, and found the baby lying in an old-fashioned basket cradle. The moment it saw her, it stopped crying and smiled.

It was a lovely fat ghostling baby. William, shining the torch for Harriet, could not see it at all, but he was forced to admit it was there when Harriet thrust its warm, curly head against his fingers. She carried it downstairs to her room, and cuddled it and loved it and thought of little else for days and days. Sometimes she fed it on bread and milk, but ghost babies do well enough living on air.

Now she had her baby ghost and William had his skeleton. Their mother could not make them out at all.

'My children have almost *too* much imagination!' she complained to her friends. 'They play all day long with imaginary companions! Harriet pretends she is looking after a baby! She pushes it out in an old doll's pram that she hasn't looked at for years. She is really much too big to push a doll's pram. And William carries around a polythene shopping bag as if there was something precious inside it! Perhaps they are geniuses! I don't know!'

So here they were, going to Miss Meadie's party by bus, since it was difficult to take either the baby or the skeleton on a bicycle, and William was a little sulky because he had not wanted to go, but Harriet had persuaded him it would be hard luck on the skeleton if he didn't.

Harriet had been to visit Miss Meadie just once more, after she had found the baby.

'Good!' said Miss Meadie. 'It is just in time to come to my ghost party.'

Harriet stared.

'I give a ghost party every year,' Miss Meadie went on. 'On Hallowe'en, of course! The patrons like it and it keeps the ghosts off the streets. You can come!'

'And William?' asked Harriet.

'If that is the skeleton boy, then of course he can come,' said Miss Meadie. 'But don't tell all and sundry. I only want people *with* ghosts, not people without, and I don't want newspapermen or the general public. They might win the game and that would be a pity.'

'What game?' asked Harriet at once.

'Why, the Wishing Bean game!' said Miss Meadie. 'The darling ghosties look forward to it all the year round.

You see, after everybody has eaten all they can, I bring on a great dish of hot spiced curry, very hot and very spicy, and somewhere in it there is hidden a little round yellow bean. Everybody eats and eats and eats in the hope that the bean will be found in their portion, because if it is . . . '

'What?' asked Harriet, excited.

'They have a wish!' said Miss Meadie. 'And the wish comes true. Always. Just that one wish, at that one moment in the year.'

'What do they usually wish for?' asked Harriet, wondering what a ghost could desire on such an occasion.

'You never can tell!' said Miss Meadie, shaking her head. 'The very strangest things! There was a cavalier – you know, the kind of fellow who carries his head under his arm. We were all so pleased when he got the bean. We felt sure he would wish to have his head put back on his shoulders again. Well, wouldn't you? But not a bit of it! He wished for a really dashing hat with white feathers in it! He said he would be able to admire it much more easily if he wore it underneath his arm.'

'What else did they wish for?' asked Harriet.

'Well, there was a lady who had been drowned,' said Miss Meadie. 'She wished for a modern permanent wave, because they did not have them in her day. But sometimes it isn't the ghosties who get the bean. Sometimes it's the patrons, and some are very selfish. They wish for cruises in the Mediterranean and things like that which their dear ones can't take part in. One of them wanted a flat in Paris. His ghost couldn't go *there* – it couldn't understand French! So selfish, wasn't it?'

'Can they wish for just anything?' asked Harriet.

'Just anything!' said Miss Meadie. 'And when I think of all the wasted opportunities, I sometimes think I'll never give a party again.'

Harriet immediately began to think what she would wish for if she got the bean at Miss Meadie's party, and she decided on a really beautiful perambulator for the baby, that she could push around without being told that she was really too old for a doll's pram.

'I think it is very kind indeed of you to give a party for us and our ghosts,' she told Miss Meadie. 'Everyone must be very grateful to you.'

'Well, we have our enemies, of course,' said Miss Meadie. 'No doubt you read the advertisement in the paper under the heading "Miscellaneous"?'

Harriet had not. Miss Meadie handed her the paper.

'"Let me solve your psychic problems",' Harriet read aloud. 'Is it advertising medicine?'

'*Psychic*, not *physic!*' said Miss Meadie, fondling the two ghost cats that were sparring for her attention. 'Read on!'

'"Exorcizer guarantees to rid you of pests, black-beetles and all unnatural phenomena for a moderate fee. Apply: Rid-a-Ghoster, Telephone 0000007. All correspondence answered."'

'How silly!' said Harriet. 'I bet he can't do it!'

'Don't be too sure,' said Miss Meadie. '*We* love our ghosties, so they are safe with us, but hatred is very dangerous. It destroys. And I don't believe that Mr Rid-a-Ghoster is a true exorcist or he wouldn't do it for money. A real exorcist helps our friends into another world with love and tenderness, if they really want to go. *He* does it with their consent and co-operation. This man is just out to make money.'

'Well, he shan't have *my* little ghost, or William's!' said Harriet firmly.

The bus shook and jolted. William's skeleton got out of the bag and sat beside him on the seat, since there were very few passengers. The baby slept contentedly in Harriet's basket. She kept peeping at it to see if it was awake or not.

'What have you got in there, love?' asked the woman sitting next to her. 'Is it a kitten?'

'No,' said Harriet, going red.

'Is it a bunny, then?'

'No!' said Harriet, furious with herself for having made loving noises to the baby ghost. 'It's nothing at all!' she added firmly.

The lady was too inquisitive to let that pass. She leaned across Harriet as if to peer inside the basket. The baby woke up and cried.

'Look! It's nothing at all!' Harriet repeated defiantly. She thrust the basket under the lady's nose and saw the look of surprise that came into her face when she realized that, in fact, it appeared perfectly empty. William, who had been dozing, woke up with a jerk.

'Why's it crying?' he asked loudly.

The skeleton kicked him.

'Ouch!' William said, rubbing his shin. 'You didn't have to do that! I wish I hadn't brought you!'

The lady sat back, looking perfectly astonished, and the bus, arriving at a bus stop, ground to a halt. William, still rubbing his shin, was avenged when a new passenger sat down solidly on top of his skeleton, though only Harriet could see its indignant limbs sticking out on either side of the tweed-coated gentleman who had almost obliterated it.

And suddenly she noticed that the newcomer himself was not without his attendant sprites. His pockets were full of small poltergeists, busy unpicking his buttons, unravelling his pipe tobacco and making holes in his handkerchief. The man seemed to be only half aware of them, but Harriet could see that he was a worried person.

Before the bus restarted, a cloppetting of hooves down the road brought Harriet's head round with a jerk. A man was running at full speed to catch the bus, holding by a rope an enormous grey mare with fiery eyes and the sort of transparency about it that Harriet had long since learned to associate with phantoms. William looked round too, but when the man had leapt on board he took no further notice. He was stroking the skeleton's hand as it clung to his knee for reassurance. Harriet saw that the horse was attempting to board the bus as well.

'Step along please!' the conductor said, as the man stopped to buy his ticket.

The horse reared up and came down with one of its forefeet fair and square on the conductor's toe. Harriet winced, but the conductor went on punching the ticket as if nothing had happened, and then moved away down the bus, while the man tied the horse's rope to the rail inside the door and sat down on the other side of Harriet, breathing heavily. The horse's hooves pounded along behind, breaking into a gallop as the bus gathered speed.

The horse's owner was staring across at William and William's neighbour as if his eyes would pop out of his head. Harriet realized that the man had noticed something, but just how much she could not tell. To test him, she opened the basket, and the baby began to cry. Harriet took it in her arms.

'Cor! Nice little kid!' said the man admiringly, and then, in a tone of relief: 'You going to Miss Meadie's party, then?'

Harriet realized that her neighbour too had the gift of seeing Other Things. She nodded.

'Didn't see you there last year,' the man went on conversationally. 'Is that your brother across the way? He's like you. That chap beside him, what's sitting on all those bones, he's a funny one, he is. He's stark staring terrified of those little tiddlers playing up and down his weskit. He brings 'em every year hoping Miss Meadie will get rid of 'em for him, but she loves 'em, bless her heart. Now I wouldn't mind a snuff-out powder for my horse! He's a right nuisance, kicking his stall to pieces when the moon is full and when hounds go by – well! You can't hold him! He's after 'em, and every dog of 'em puts its tail between its legs and hares for home! No wonder all the foxes run straight for my place! You can see 'em laughing! But the Hunt thinks I does it on purpose.'

'Bad luck!' said Harriet.

'Anyway, I've had enough,' said the man. 'This year I'm getting rid of him. There's a chap coming to Miss Meadie's party that can settle things for good and all. An exorcist, he's called. I believe he's a dab hand at ghosts.'

Harriet was just opening her mouth to say that Miss Meadie would never invite anyone like that to her party, when the bus stopped again, a new passenger got on, and immediately, in front of Harriet's very eyes, every ghost went out like a light.

The baby, which had been kicking and chuckling, began to cry bitterly, and Harriet rocked it to and fro to comfort it.

Opposite, the skeleton somehow eased itself out from beneath the body of the man on top and folded itself back into William's bag. The little poltergeists became as flat as shadows and disappeared inside various pockets. Their patron, who seemed to have even less awareness than William, remained staring straight ahead of him with his hands on his knees, while the newcomer walked quietly to the very front of the bus and sat down. He wore a wide-brimmed black hat, and a long black coat. His ears stuck out slightly, and he had a long, thin nose.

Harriet was acutely aware of something wrong about him. He looked just horrid. The horse-owner suddenly noticed him too.

'That's the bloke!' he muttered to Harriet. 'That's the Rid-a-Ghost man! He's going to do quite a bit of business at the party, he told me. I'm not the only one wanting to get rid of a ghostie. Just look at my old grey mare there! Her's got the message!'

Outside the bus, in fact, the grey mare, with her ears laid flat back against her head, could be seen straining against the rope that pulled her. Faintly, at William's feet, the skeleton's teeth could be heard chattering inside the carrier bag.

While the horse's owner moved down the bus to speak confidentially to the uncanny stranger, Harriet noticed that the knot securing the horse's rope to the rail was on the point of coming undone.

'Hold the baby a minute!' she said to William, dumping it on his knees.

'It'll wet,' said William gingerly.

'No, it won't, you twit! It will only feel as if it does!' said Harriet, dashing up the bus. She seized the rope just as the horse was about to break away, and tied it securely to the rail.

'Hey!' shouted the conductor. 'Don't get off before the bus stops!' But the bus was already slowing down.

Nearly everybody got off at the stop nearest to Miss Meadie's. Harriet got off first. She flew up the drive to warn Miss Meadie about the unwelcome visitor who was about to invade the party. But Miss Meadie, busy receiving a score of invited guests, had little time to listen to what Harriet was saying.

Patron after patron, ghost after ghost, were being welcomed into the hall and shown to their seats at a long table which was piled with all kinds of delicious food.

When everyone was in their places, Harriet saw to her great relief that the Rid-a-Ghoster was not, after all, among them. Perhaps his courage had failed him in the face of such a happy throng of friends and phantoms, now raising their glasses to toast Miss Meadie, and drinking to the Past, the Happy Past and the Past Again.

Watching the enthusiasm of ghosts and patrons alike, Harriet found it hard to believe that any of these loyal guests could be planning to jettison their phantom friends before the evening was out. She clutched the ghostling baby more closely to her, and noticed that William and his skeleton were fondly sharing a dish of trifle, and clinking spoons.

The evening passed with feasting and music, the excitement growing more intense as one phantom after another burst into song, and everybody joined in. The horse neighed after every verse, the skeleton danced a fandango on the table, the poltergeists pelted everyone with popcorn and Miss Meadie called them her naughty little piglets.

Then at last she clapped her hands, and silence fell.

'We have now come to the climax of our feast!' announced Miss Meadie. 'I shall bring in the dish of the Wishing Bean. You all know what to do! Each one will serve himself with as large a portion as he is still able to eat, and in one of the portions will be found a small, round bean! Whoever finds it can wish one wish aloud, and that wish is bound to come true. Blessings on you all, and may the lucky one's dreams be realized!'

There was a burst of applause as she rose to leave the table, followed by the phantom butler and several dogs and cats, some quite transparent and others with the normal complement of heads, tails and whiskers. Harriet watched her go with mounting excitement. The great moment of the day had arrived! And everyone, *everyone*, had a chance to win. Even the baby would have to be woken up to taste its portion.

But when she looked back again at the table, the Rid-a-Ghoster was sitting in Miss Meadie's chair. Where he had come from nobody could say, but he did not give them time to wonder.

'Friends!' he shouted, leaping to his feet. 'The fun and games are over! The phantoms have had their day! Life is not a party for the dead-and-gone before! Life goes on, tomorrow and the next day and the next, and the one after! Do we want to remain in the thraldom of our hauntings? Do we want to hear again the cryings in the dark, the knockings on the door, the trippings-up and the trippings-in? Do we want our cats' fur standing on end? Our dogs crouching in corners with their tails between their legs? Our plates and cups and saucers hurled about our heads? Do we want to be controlled all our lives long by these wretched manifestations we call ghosts, for want of a better name for them? No! No! Many of you have already come to me for help in ridding you of these pests. Many of you have asked me to meet you here tonight in order to destroy these – these black-beetles! Pah! But I am your friend! Trust in the Rid-a-Ghoster and you shall be freed from your fears! Five pounds please, paid in advance!'

Harriet sat horrified. She saw some of the patrons, looking sheepishly at each other. Two or three put their hands into their pockets, searching for money. A few pound notes were already passing into the Rid-a-Ghoster's greedy palm.

The kitchen door was flung open and Miss Meadie appeared, bearing a steaming dish. She gave one look at the Rid-a-Ghoster and banged the dish down on the table in front of him.

'My seat, if you please,' she said curtly.

Unwillingly, the Rid-a-Ghoster gave it up to her. 'I remain at your service!' he announced to the table at large. 'Whoever wishes to avail themselves of my powers may come with me into the next room. Bring your phantoms with you. Those who have already paid will be served first.'

He was about to retire when he saw that the attention of the whole company was riveted on the Wishing Dish. Nobody wanted to lose their chance of finding the wonderful bean. Those who wished to be exorcized decided to have it done afterwards.

Reluctantly the Rid-a-Ghoster sat down among the rest, and before he could be prevented, he snatched an ample portion of the dish's contents as it circled the table.

The bean was too small to be seen with the naked eye, but Miss Meadie assured everyone that they would know it when they found it on their tongues.

An atmosphere of intense expectation filled the room. Everybody wanted to find the precious bean, and one could almost see the shadows of the various wishes flitting round the table.

Harriet was terribly anxious. There were at least forty chances to one against her winning the bean. She did not even expect to get it. Supposing William got it? If he were sitting nearer to her she could tell him what to wish for, but that was not allowed.

Suppose the horse got it? Nobody would even know. It had swallowed its portion already, and the bean might have gone down with it as far as anyone could tell. Suppose one of the poltergeists got it? They were bound to do something silly with it – they were that sort of person. Suppose the baby got it? But, after the first mouthful, it went back to sleep and Harriet ate its share herself.

The company chewed on. The hall was very quiet now, everyone glancing covertly at his neighbour, dreading any hesitation that might signal the finding of the bean.

The worst thing that could happen, Harriet decided, was that the Rid-a-Ghoster should get it. He was quite capable of destroying every phantom in the room if he did. He ate with concentration, carefully chewing every mouthful to the end and sometimes looking up to catch Harriet's eye upon him.

'If he gets it,' Harriet thought, 'I know he will get rid of the baby and I'll never see it again. I couldn't bear it! I'd just die! And Miss Meadie will die, too, if he destroys all the darling ghosts that she loves so much . . .'

Even Miss Meadie was chewing desperately, keeping her eye meanwhile on the Rid-a-Ghost man. She was almost willing him not to find the bean.

All of a sudden, the Rid-a-Ghoster stopped eating, and choked.

The whole table froze, stopped their own chewing, and looked at him. The Rid-a-Ghoster leaned over the table, coughing and spluttering while the skeleton kindly beat him on the back between the shoulder blades.

The Rid-a-Ghoster searched for a handkerchief in his pocket and put it to his lips.

'He's got it!' Harriet said to herself, feeling quite faint. 'He's got it . . . he's got the bean!'

At that moment her own tongue met something hard inside her mouth. She pushed it impatiently aside and was about to swallow it when the piercing realization of what it might be, of what it actually *was*, arrested her in the middle of her swallow. Quickly she put her hand to her mouth and removed a tiny, hard round bean from the back of her tongue. Even when she saw it lying in the palm of her hand, she could hardly believe it.

'I've got the bean!' Harriet announced.

Her first feeling was of such pure relief that she wanted to burst into tears. The Rid-a-Ghoster, whatever else he might do, could not now destroy them all. Then all the wishes that she had ever wished for came crowding into her head, wishes for her family, wishes for herself, wishes for the people.

But the wish that came bursting from her lips even before she found words to say it went ringing round the table, and everyone stared and listened, and listened and stared again, as Harriet shouted:

'I wish that all the ghosts in this room were real people for ever and ever and ever!'

A hush fell upon Miss Meadie's table, and one by one each guest looked at one another. Nobody said a word, until the horse's owner got to his feet, remarking: 'That's a good horse, that one is! And I reckon it's about time he carried me home!' He left the room quietly, and they heard him clopping away down the drive!

There came a popping sound from the direction of the gentleman with the poltergeists, followed by another and another, as if small fireworks were exploding. He got up from the table and left, quite alone. There wasn't a sign of anything fussing about in his pockets and he seemed much calmer.

'Exactly!' murmured Miss Meadie half-aloud. 'I never did understand about poltergeists . . . '

The cavalier with the feathered hat was now a smartly dressed Member of Parliament. He said goodbye to Miss Meadie, explaining that he had to be in the House in the morning. The drowned lady was talking about sailing to someone who had looked very much like a pirate a few moments ago. They were arranging to sail around the world together. A tonsured monk was now a bishop, returning thanks for the meal they had all received, while a small grey lady left early, saying she had duties in the

Public Library and would put Miss Meadie's books on psychic research on one side for her to collect in the morning.

The strangest transformation of all was William's skeleton. It had completely disappeared. By William's side was a charming young woman who was cuddling Harriet's baby. 'It is my baby,' she told Harriet. 'It always was. But you can come and play with it whenever you like.'

Harriet realized that this was for the best. A real live baby that everyone could interfere with was much less convenient than a phantom. Besides which, a real live baby would be even more enchanting to play with than a ghostling.

'Do you mind about your skeleton being a *her*?' she asked William.

'No,' he replied. 'If it can't be a skeleton I don't care what it is,' and he turned away.

The Rid-a-Ghoster was escaping through the door when several people prevented him, and took back their money. He did not even have enough left for his bus fare, and had to walk back to the town.

Harriet turned to Miss Meadie. She was feeling very guilty at the ways things had turned out. 'I'm terribly sorry,' she said. 'I seem to have taken away all your friends at once.'

Suddenly she noticed that Miss Meadie herself looked quite different from the Miss Meadie she had known before.

'It doesn't matter,' Miss Meadie said quietly. 'I was really getting tired of being a ghost myself. I'd rather be a human being. I'm going to have a home for cats and dogs that people have deserted. Goodnight, Harriet! I'm glad you won the bean. Come and see me sometimes, and I hope you enjoyed the party.'

And Harriet and William went home by bus, quite alone.

Dog's Dinner
Lynne Hackles

It was me who broke Fonsie's dish. Doesn't sound like much, does it? But because of that one mistake Fonsie is now starving and I could end up with the weight of a dog's death on my shoulders.

It happened the day we were moving into our new house. Nobody asked me to shift any heavy furniture or precious wineglasses or bone china. Nothing like that. All I was left in charge of was a few odds and ends crammed into the boot of the car.

'Bring that lot in for me, son,' said Dad.

I stared into the boot. With a bit of forward planning I reckoned the entire contents could be carried in one go. So much for Mum always saying my head would never save my legs.

My Lazy Head told me, 'If we put Mum's handbag on the left shoulder and perch those few books, the dog food, the tin-opener and the dish on top of the washing-basket, we'll only have to do one journey.' Sounded good to me.

If I'd used my Thinking Head it would have said, 'You must be joking. That bag's mega-sized and about the same weight as a sack of coal. Mum's got everything in there, her make-up, chequebooks, address books, notebooks, library books, chocolate bars, Everton mints, sherbet lemons. Do you want me to continue? And you think you can carry it while the rest of the stuff does a balancing act on top of the washing basket? Three journeys would be sensible.'

Instead of listening I slung the bag over my right shoulder, heaved up the basket in both arms and closed the boot of the car with my nose.

The new house was on an unadopted road, a road that no one cared for and no one had ever bothered to build properly. More of a track really. A striped track. Brown, green, brown. A stripe of green grass bordered on either side by strips of thick brown mud. Glutinous chocolate mud. Mud of the Grade 1 Slide and Stick variety and deep enough for any fussy hippo to wallow in. A dozen hazardous steps and I would have crossed that no man's land and reached the safety of the garden path leading to our new home. But some things are not meant to be.

At the sixth step the bag dislodged itself.

The strap was used to being firmly wedged between Mum's neck and her shoulder pads and my sweat-shirt didn't have shoulder pads. The bag, sensing freedom, swung gracefully off my shoulder and gathered speed as it cruised over my chest on a pre-plotted course towards my crotch. Not wanting to end up as a soprano I swerved as though I was on the rugby field. The washing-basket saved my crotch. Nothing saved the washing-basket. My trainers slipped in the mud and down I went, on one knee. The basket complete with its assorted topping catapulted through the air and crash-landed in the front garden.

What the estate agent had described as an herbaceous border now bloomed with paperbacks and tins of Pal. A selection of Dad's shirts had escaped from the bottom of the basket to drape themselves over a prickly bush near the front door.

As I picked up the bits and pieces I congratulated myself. Things could have been worse. The mega-bag could have burst. Then I spotted it. The catastrophe. It must have hit the wall of the house with some force to be in so many pieces.

Fonsie's dish was shattered.

It was a very old dish. Not an antique. Not valuable. Just plain brown, oval and ugly. But Fonsie loved it. He had

never known another dish. Every morning for as far back as he could remember his breakfast biscuits had materialized in that dish. Every evening, as he lay on my bed having his pre-dinner nap, he would be woken by the sound of brown ironstone slapping on to formica – there was no other sound in his world like it – and he would know that another tin of meaty chunks had come to the end of its shelf-life. Now he was going to have to get used to a new dish.

'He can have this old saucer for tonight,' said Mum mashing rabbit and carrots over a garland of crimson roses.

Fonsie turned up his nose in disgust. It was as if he had X-ray vision and could see the flowers beneath the meat. With his tail tucked so far between his legs it touched his stomach he slouched back to the fire and the television.

'Tomorrow you can buy him a new one,' said Mum. 'Out of your own money.'

I didn't get the cheapest. It must have been something to do with guilt feelings. The way my dog had trotted down the stairs that morning expecting his breakfast biscuits to be waiting for him. And they were waiting but not in the right dish. I'd picked out a biscuit of each shape and each colour and arranged them on the Wallace and Gromit plate Gran had bought me for Christmas but it wasn't the same. Fonsie looked at the plate and the biscuits and then at me and I could see the question in those sorrowful brown eyes. 'Where's *my* dish?'

The label in the pet shop said the new dish was unbreakable and hygienic. It was round, bright blue and plastic and came complete with a sucker on its bottom. Remember the sucker things on the end of toy arrows? When they're fired from the bow they stick to the wall or the television screen or between Gran's eyes. Well, Fonsie's new dish had one of those so that once it had descended to the kitchen floor it was immovable. No matter how intense the snuffling and chomping, dinner remained static. He'll love it, I thought as money changed hands. No more chasing his meals around the room.

He hated it. Took one look and decided that blue plastic was far inferior to brown ironstone, even if it was brimming over with meaty chunks and didn't go walkabouts.

I tried to explain about it being a present, being unbreakable, being hygienic, everything it said in the sales blurb on the label but he only turned his back on me and the dish and went to bed for his after-dinner nap – except he hadn't had any dinner.

'And the colour matches your lead,' I called after him but he didn't want to know.

He didn't touch the next morning's breakfast either.

'Leave him alone,' said Dad. 'He'll eat when he's hungry.' That's what he says to Mum when I refuse meals. But I just leave my stuffed cabbage leaves and nip out for a Big Mac instead. I wondered how long it would be before Fonsie took himself off to the nearest burger bar.

Three days later he was still on hunger strike and disappearing before my very eyes. I could picture him, bones sticking out through his moulting coat, trudging across the common in search of an RSPCA inspector. I was seriously worried.

'Please try a bit,' I begged, longing to see him back to normal, scoffing away, snout down, bum in the air.

After a week I resorted to sitting on the kitchen floor and spoon feeding him direct from the tin. It worked but was time-consuming and definitely not a life-long solution. The procedure needed lots of patience on both sides. I could never master the amount of food one small terrier required on his cereal spoon and the terrier couldn't make up his mind whether to suck or bite it.

The guilt trip was doing my head in. Every time our eyes met I knew what Fonsie was thinking. 'You broke *my* dish. This is all your fault.'

A fortnight has passed since Broken Dish Day. Fonsie is surviving on toast crusts and other tit-bits passed under cover of the tablecloth. He's looking thin but I've had to leave him at home on his own because I promised to help out at the school's car-boot sale.

The parents are trying to sell off the junk they don't want in the new house. They don't see me slope off because they're too busy trying to off-load my old roller boots on to some little kid.

In the canteen I grab a coke and sit next to my mate Dave and before I know it we are discussing canine spoon-feeding techniques.

'Why don't you get rid of the plastic dish and find him something else?' says Dave.

If only it was that easy. 'I've tried everything from cracked saucers to Royal Worcester. You see,' I explain, 'his last dish was different, something special. I need another one the same.'

'Or something equally as gross,' suggests Dave. 'Let's see what's on offer.'

We leave the canteen together and enter the spirit of the occasion by becoming avid car-booters searching for a bargain. There are plenty of dishes to choose from, large and small, but they are either too pretty or too tasteful.

'Any idea what we're looking for?' asks Dave.

'No, but I'll know it when I see it.'

He discards a chipped pink floral thing and picks up a pale green chamber pot. I shake my head.

And then Miss Chalk heaves a cardboard box from the back of her Range Rover and plonks it on to the sagging trestle-table in front of her. 'Bargains,' she shouts. 'Everything must go. Fifty pence an item.'

I dig, elbow deep, into the box and pull out a handful of lace-edged hankies. Back in for another go and this time I emerge with a glossy white ashtray, slightly smaller than a hospital bed-pan. Around its sides in fluorescent green are the words WHISKEY FLAKE, followed by READY RUBBED in jaffa orange.

It's certainly ugly enough and should be unique as a dog's feeding bowl.

'What do you think?' I pass the ashtray to Dave who, like a connoisseur, twists it in his hands, reading the sides. He scrapes at a green W with his thumbnail. 'It'll take some time but this should scratch off,' he tells me.

I carry it home with crossed fingers, bathe it in hot Fairy liquid bubbles and gently pat it dry on kitchen paper before reaching for the Beef and Liver.

I call Fonsie from his afternoon nap and hear his clattering descent of the, as yet, uncarpeted stairs.

'Look what I've got for you.'

He circles the ashtray, giving it a nudge with his nose. It skitters a yard to the north-east. Fonsie follows. I hold my breath. And then, without the aid of a spoon, Fonsie eats his first proper meal in a fortnight.

'I'll spend tomorrow morning scratching that writing off,' I promise him.

In the middle of the night I wake up. Something is niggling at the back of my mind.

I sit up in bed and switch on the light. Fonsie, his little belly swollen from a large dinner, blinks and rolls over on to my feet.

'I've just thought of something,' I say.

Fonsie burps and stares at me.

'You can't read.'

Cuts
Russell Hoban

Cuts! Don't talk to me about cuts. With London Transport and the NHS you expect it, but dreams for God's sake! I mean your own personal dreams that you dream in your own personal sleep in the privacy of your own home.

My name is Higgins, Clarence Higgins. You want chapter and verse, I'll give you chapter and verse. One night I was in this dream – not even a first showing but a repeat. We'd got to the part where I was on the Wimbledon train and I saw someone reading an *Evening Standard* and the headline was HIGGINS MISSING. I moved closer for a better look and there was nothing else on the front page, nothing at all under the headline. The first time I had this dream there was a bit of story, continued on Page Two, about how I went missing and what led up to it – I remember that quite well.

'Excuse me, please,' I said to the man reading it. I took the paper and turned it round to see what he'd been reading and the spread facing him was perfectly blank! Not a word on it. 'Look at that,' I said to him. He was the same man who'd been reading the paper in this dream the first time round. 'That's just not good enough, is it?' I said. 'They're not paying proper attention to detail any more. Would you mind standing up and turning around for me?' He stood up and turned around and it was as I'd suspected – the back of him was just as blank as the inside of the *Evening Standard*.

'This is too much,' I said. 'It really is too much.'

'It's no use complaining to me,' he said. 'I just go where I'm sent and do as I'm told. I mean, I'm lucky to get the work, enn I? There's lot of us has had nothing at all for weeks and weeks.'

'Lucky to get the work! You're only half a man – the back of you is a total blank and you're just going to accept that, are you?'

'What can I do about it?'

'Who's the Secretary of State for Dreams?'

'I haven't a clue. I always thought it was a local authority thing,' he said, and vanished as I woke up.

'Did you hear that?' I said to Gladys, she's my wife. 'They cut me off in the middle of a conversation, just like that.'

'It was only a dream, Clarence.'

'Only a dream! Everything's falling apart and you lie there and say it's only a dream. Now that I think of it, there weren't even any sound effects in that tube train, nothing but that miserable bit of dialogue. And nothing visible outside the carriage windows. Nobody cares about doing things right any more.'

Later that day I rang up the Borough of Hammersmith and Fulham. 'Who's in charge of dreams?' I said.

'I'll see if I can find out,' said the telephonist. I held while she made her enquiries. When she came back on to the line she said, 'There doesn't seem to be anyone. Are you awake or asleep?'

'Awake.'

'Try again later when you're asleep. They may be able to help you then.'

Easier said than done: every night in my dreams I rang them up and every time I got an engaged signal. And the phone boxes I used! Some of them were only two-dimensional, with telephones like pieces of flat cardboard. The streets were filled with fronts and sides of cars and buses – if you didn't look at them from a certain angle the illusion of reality was gone. And the people! Profiles only, most of them. Full-face here and there. I knew better than to look at their backs as they passed. All right, I said to myself, we'll see about this. When the going gets tough, the tough dream a visit to the Town Hall.

I thought it best to avoid public transport in this dream; I hailed a sort of fake-looking cab, and when I was in it I saw that there was no driver and I had to keep pushing with one foot to make it go, like a child's scooter.

When I finally got to the Town Hall I asked the receptionist for Dreams and she said, 'Third floor'. I didn't trust the lifts; I went two at a time up stairs that disappeared behind me until I found *Dream Planning and Development*. There were several people at drawing tables and one pale profile of a man walking about in a supervisory sort of way. I tried to stay full-face but I could feel myself going flat and sideways.

'All right, you lot,' I said. 'What's going on here?'

'What's the problem?' said Mr Profile.

'You know jolly well what the problem is! Look around you at the way this dream is being conducted. You should be ashamed of yourselves.'

'What's your postcode?'

I told him.

'Name?'

I told him.

He went to a computer terminal and danced his fingers over the keyboard. I looked over his shoulder at the screen but all I could see was a row of Xs. 'Ah, well!' he said. 'I'm surprised you've been getting any dreams at all.'

'Why?' I could feel a coldness in the pit of my stomach.

'Well, you know they've halved our funding this year and we've had to cut back on everything. What I'm saying is, we've shut down the whole dream operation on your street and you've been made redundant.'

'Thanks very much,' I said. 'I'll see myself out.'

But I couldn't. No stairs, no lifts – just the merest sketch of a Town Hall interior and it went all dim and silent. Sometimes I'd catch a glimmer of someone but even when their mouths moved I couldn't hear anything and then they'd be gone. That was how long ago? Days? Months? Years? I'm not sure.

I don't know how much longer I can hold out here. I've tried to send this dream to Gladys but I'm not strong enough and in any case the dreams aren't running in our street any more. All I can hope for is that she'll move to some place where they are and then maybe she can dream me home.

But I don't know – it looks pretty bad from where I stand. Not that I'm standing, actually. If I wake up, or if you wake up – I'm not sure which – I expect these words will disappear.

Wunderpants
Paul Jennings

My Dad is not a bad sort of bloke. There are plenty who are much worse. But he does rave on a bit, like if you get muddy when you are catching frogs, or rip your pants when you are building a tree hut. Stuff like that.

Mostly we understand each other and I can handle him. What he doesn't know doesn't hurt him. If he knew that I kept Snot, my pet rabbit, under the bed, he wouldn't like it; so I don't tell him. That way he is happy, I am happy and Snot is happy.

There are only problems when he finds out what has been going on. Like the time that I wanted to see *Mad Max II*. The old man said it was a bad movie – too much blood and guts.

'It's too violent,' he said.

'But, Dad, that's not fair. All the other kids are going. I'll be the only one in the school who hasn't seen it.' I went on and on like this. I kept nagging. In the end he gave in – he wasn't a bad old boy. He usually let me have what I wanted after a while. It was easy to get around him.

The trouble started the next morning. He was cleaning his teeth in the bathroom, making noises, humming and gurgling – you know the sort of thing. Suddenly he stopped. Everything went quiet. Then he came into the kitchen. There was toothpaste all around his mouth; he looked like a mad tiger. He was frothing at the mouth.

'What's this?' he said. He was waving his toothbrush about. 'What's this on my toothbrush?' Little grey hairs were sticking out of it. 'How did these hairs get on my toothbrush? Did you have my toothbrush, David?'

He was starting to get mad. I didn't know whether to own up or not. Parents always tell you that if you own up they will let you off. They say that they won't do anything if you arc honest – no punishment.

I decided to give it a try. 'Yes,' I said. 'I used it yesterday.'

He still had toothpaste on his mouth. He couldn't talk properly. 'What are these little grey hairs?' he asked.

'I used it to brush my pet mouse,' I answered.

'Your what?' he screamed.

'My mouse.'

He started jumping up and down and screaming. He ran around in circles holding his throat, then he ran into the bathroom and started washing his mouth out. There was a lot of splashing and gurgling. He was acting like a madman.

I didn't know what all the fuss was about. All that yelling just over a few mouse hairs.

After a while he came back into the kitchen. He kept opening and shutting his mouth as if he could taste something bad. He had a mean look in his eye – real mean.

'What are you thinking of?' he yelled at the top of his voice. 'Are you crazy or something? Are you trying to kill me? Don't you know that mice carry germs? They are filthy things. I'll probably die of some terrible disease.'

He went on and on like this for ages. Then he said, 'And don't think that you are going to see *Mad Max II*. You can sit at home and think how stupid it is to brush a mouse with someone else's toothbrush.'

I went back to my room to get dressed. Dad just didn't understand about that mouse. It was a special mouse, a very special mouse indeed. It was going to make me a lot of money: fifty dollars, in fact. Every year there was a mouse race in Smith's barn. The prize was fifty dollars.

And my mouse, Swift Sam, had a good chance of winning. But I had to look after him. That's why I brushed him with a toothbrush.

I knew that Swift Sam could beat every other mouse except one. There was one mouse I wasn't sure about. It was called Mugger and it was owned by Scrag Murphy, the toughest kid in the town. I had never seen his mouse, but I knew it was fast. Scrag Murphy fed it on a special diet.

That is what I was thinking about as I dressed. I went over to the cupboard to get a pair of underpants. There were none there. 'Hey, Mum,' I yelled out. 'I am out of underpants.'

Mum came into the room holding something terrible. Horrible. It was a pair of home-made underpants. 'I made these for you, David,' she said. 'I bought the material at the Op Shop. There was just the right amount of material for one pair of underpants.'

'I'm not wearing those,' I told her. 'No way. Never.'

'What's wrong with them?' said Mum. She sounded hurt.

'They're pink,' I said. 'And they've got little pictures of fairies on them. I couldn't wear them. Everyone would laugh. I would be the laughing stock of the school.'

Underpants with fairies on them and pink. I nearly freaked out. I thought about what Scrag Murphy would say if he ever heard about them. I went red just thinking about it.

Just then Dad poked his head into the room. He still had that mean look in his eye. He was remembering the toothbrush. 'What's going on now?' he asked in a black voice.

'Nothing,' I said. 'I was just thanking Mum for making me these nice underpants.' I pulled on the fairy pants and quickly covered them up with my jeans. At least no one else would know I had them on. That was one thing to be thankful for.

The underpants felt strange. They made me tingle all over. And my head felt light. There was something not quite right about those underpants – and I am not talking about the fairies.

I had breakfast and went out to the front gate. Pete was waiting for me. He is my best mate; we always walk to school together. 'Have you got your running shoes?' he asked.

'Oh no,' I groaned. 'I forgot. It's the cross country race today.' I went back and got my running shoes. I came back out walking very slowly. I was thinking about the race. I would have to go the changing-rooms and get changed in front of Scrag Murphy and all the other boys. They would all laugh their heads off when they saw my fairy underpants.

We walked through the park on the way to school. There was a big lake in the middle. 'Let's chuck some stones,' said Pete. 'See who can throw the furthest.' I didn't even answer. I was feeling weak in the stomach. 'What's the matter with you?' he asked. 'You look like death warmed up.'

I looked around. There was no one else in the park. 'Look at this,' I said. I undid my fly and showed Pete the underpants. His eyes bugged out like organ stops; then he started to laugh. He fell over on the grass and laughed his silly head off. Tears rolled down his cheeks. He really thought it was funny. Some friend.

After a while Pete stopped laughing. 'You poor thing,' he said. 'What are you going to do? Scrag Murphy and the others will never let you forget it.'

We started throwing stones into the lake. I didn't try very hard. My heart wasn't in it. 'Hey,' said Pete. 'That was a good shot. It went right over to the other side.' He was right. The stone had reached the other side of the lake. No one had ever done that before; it was too far.

I picked up another stone. This time I threw as hard as I could. The stone went right over the lake and disappeared over some trees. 'Wow,' yelled Pete. 'That's the best shot I've ever seen. No one can throw that far.' He looked at me in a funny way.

My skin was all tingling. 'I feel strong,' I said. 'I feel as if I can do anything.' I went over to a park bench. It was a large concrete one. I lifted it up with one hand. I held it high over my head. I couldn't believe it.

Pete just stood there with his mouth hanging open. He couldn't believe it either. I felt great. I jumped for joy. I sailed high into the air. I went up three metres. 'What a jump,' yelled Pete.

My skin was still tingling. Especially under the underpants. 'It's the underpants,' I said. 'The underpants are giving me strength.' I grinned. 'They are not underpants. They are *wunderpants*.'

'Super Jocks,' said Pete. We both started cackling like a couple of hens. We laughed until our sides ached.

I told Pete not to tell anyone about the wunderpants. We decided to keep it a secret. Nothing much happened until the cross-country race that afternoon. All the boys went to the changing-room to put on their running gear. Scrag Murphy was there. I tried to get into my shorts without him seeing my wunderpants, but it was no good. He noticed them as soon as I dropped my jeans.

'Ah ha,' he shouted. 'Look at baby britches. Look at his fairy pants.' Everyone looked. They all started to laugh. How embarrassing. They were all looking at the fairies on my wunderpants.

Scrag Murphy was a big, fat bloke. He was really tough. He came over and pulled the elastic on my wunderpants. Then he let it go. 'Ouch,' I said. 'Cut that out. That hurts.'

'What's the matter, little Diddums?' he said. 'Can't you take it?' He shoved me roughly against the wall. I wasn't going to let him get away with that, so I pushed him back – just a little push. He went flying across the room and crashed into the wall on the other side. I just didn't know my own strength. That little push had sent him all that way. It was the wunderpants.

Scrag Murphy looked at me with shock and surprise that soon turned to a look of hate. But he didn't say anything. No one said anything. They were all thinking I was going to get my block knocked off next time I saw Scrag Murphy.

About forty kids were running in the race. We had to run through the countryside, following markers that had been put out by the teachers. It was a hot day, so I decided to wear a pair of shorts but no top.

As soon as the starting gun went I was off like a flash. I had kept my wunderpants on and they were working really well. I went straight out to the front. I had never run so fast before. As I ran along the road I passed a man on a bike. He tried to keep up with me, but he couldn't. Then I passed a car. This was really something. This was great.

I looked behind. None of the others were in sight – I was miles ahead. The trail turned off the road and into the bush. I was running along a narrow track in the forest. After a while I came to a small creek. I was hot so I decided to have a dip. After all, the others were a long way behind; I had plenty of time. I took off my shorts and running shoes, but I left the wunderpants on. I wasn't going to part with them.

I dived into the cold water. It was refreshing. I lay on my back looking at the sky. Life was good. These

wunderpants were terrific. I would never be scared of Scrag Murphy while I had them on.

Then something started to happen – something terrible. The wunderpants started to get tight. They hurt. They were shrinking. They were shrinking smaller and smaller. The pain was awful. I had to get them off. I struggled and wriggled; they were so tight they cut into my skin. In the end I got them off, and only just in time. They shrank so small that they would only just fit over my thumb. I had a narrow escape. I could have been killed by the shrinking wunderpants.

Just then I heard voices coming. It was the others in the race. I was trapped – I couldn't get out to put on my shorts. There were girls in the race. I had to stay in the middle of the creek in the nude.

It took quite a while for all the others to run by. They were all spread out along the track. Every time I went to get out of the pool, someone else would come. After a while Pete stopped at the pool. 'What are you doing?' he said. 'Even super jocks won't help you win from this far back.'

'Keep going,' I said. 'I'll tell you about it later.' I didn't want to tell him that I was in the nude. Some girls were with him.

Pete and the girls took off along the track. A bit later the last runner arrived. It was Scrag Murphy. He couldn't run fast – he was carrying too much weight. 'Well, look at this,' he said. 'It's little Fairy Pants. And what's this we have here?' He picked up my shorts and running shoes from the bank of the creek. Then he ran off with them.

'Come back,' I screamed. 'Bring those back here.' He didn't take any notice. He just laughed and kept running.

I didn't know what to do. I didn't have a stitch of clothing. I didn't even have any shoes. I was starting to feel cold; the water was freezing. I was covered in goose pimples and my teeth were chattering. In the end I had to get out. I would have frozen to death if I stayed in the water any longer.

I went and sat on a rock in the sun and tried to think of a way to get home without being seen. It was all right in the bush. I could always hide behind a tree if someone came. But once I reached the road I would be in trouble; I couldn't just walk along the road in the nude.

Then I had an idea. I looked at the tiny underpants. I couldn't put them on, but they still might work. I put them over my thumb and jumped. It was no good. It was just an ordinary small jump. I picked up a stone and threw it. It only went a short way, not much of a throw at all. The pants were too small, and I was my weak old self again.

I lay down on the rock in the sun. Ants started to crawl over me. Then the sun went behind a cloud. I started to get cold, but I couldn't walk home – not in the raw. I felt miserable. I looked around for something to wear, but there was nothing. Just trees, bushes and grass.

I knew I would have to wait until dark. The others would all have gone home by now. Pete would think I had gone home, and my parents would think I was at his place. No one was going to come and help me.

I started to think about Scrag Murphy. He was going to pay for this. I would get him back somehow.

Time went slowly, but at last it started to grow dark. I made my way back along the track. I was in bare feet and I kept standing on stones. Branches reached out and scratched me in all sorts of painful places. Then I started to think about snakes. What if I stood on one?

There were all sorts of noises in the dark. The moon had gone in, and it was hard to see where I was going. I have to admit it: I was scared. Scared stiff. To cheer myself up I started to think about what I was going to do to Scrag Murphy. Boy, was he going to get it.

At last I came to the road. I was glad to be out of the bush. My feet were cut and bleeding and I hobbled along. Every time a car went by I had to dive into the bushes. I couldn't let myself get caught in the headlights of the cars.

I wondered what I was going to do when I reached the town. There might be people around. I broke off a branch from a bush and held it in front of my 'you know what'. It was prickly, but it was better than nothing.

By the time I reached the town it was late. There was no one around. But I had to be careful – someone might come out of a house at any minute. I ran from tree to tree and wall to wall, hiding in the shadows as I went. Lucky for me the moon was in and it was very dark.

Then I saw something that gave me an idea – a phone box. I opened the door and stepped inside. A dim light shone on my naked body. I hoped that no one was looking. I had no money, but Pete had told me that if you yell into the ear-piece they can hear you on the other end. It was worth a try. I dialled our home number. Dad answered. 'Yes,' he said.

'I'm in the nude,' I shouted. 'I've lost my clothes. Help. Help.'

'Hello, hello. Who's there?' said Dad.

I shouted at the top of my voice, but Dad just kept saying 'Hello'. He sounded cross. Then I heard him say to Mum, 'It's probably that boy up to his tricks again.' He hung up the phone.

I decided to make a run for it. It was the only way. I dropped my bush and started running. I went for my life. I reached our street without meeting a soul. I thought I was safe, but I was wrong. I crashed right into someone and sent them flying. It was old Mrs Jeeves from across the road.

'Sorry,' I said. 'Gee, I'm sorry.' I helped her stand up. She was a bit short-sighted and it was dark. She hadn't noticed that I didn't have any clothes on. Then the moon came out – the blazing moon. I tried to cover my nakedness with my hands, but it was no good.

'Disgusting,' she screeched. 'Disgusting. I'll tell your father about this.'

I ran home as fast as I could. I went in the back door and jumped into bed. I tried to pretend that I was asleep. Downstairs I could hear Mrs Jeeves yelling at Dad; then the front door closed. I heard his footsteps coming up the stairs.

Well, I really copped it. I was in big trouble. Dad went on and on. 'What are you thinking of, lad? Running around in the nude. Losing all your clothes. What will the neighbours think?' He went on like that for about a week. I couldn't tell him the truth – he wouldn't believe it. No one would. The only ones who knew the whole story were Pete and I.

Dad grounded me for a month. I wasn't allowed out of the house except to go to school. No pictures, no swimming, nothing. And no pocket money either.

It was a bad month. Very bad indeed. At school Scrag Murphy gave me a hard time. He called me 'Fairy Pants'. Everyone thought it was a great joke, and there was nothing I could do about it. He was just too big for me, and his mates were all tough guys.

'This is serious,' said Pete. 'We have to put Scrag Murphy back in his box. They are starting to call me "Friend Of Fairy Pants" now. We have to get even.'

We thought and thought but we couldn't come up with anything. Then I remembered the mouse race in

Smith's barn. 'We will win the mouse race,' I shouted. 'It's in a month's time. We can use the next month to train my mouse.'

'That's it,' said Pete. 'The prize is fifty dollars. Scrag Murphy thinks he is going to win. It will really get up his nose if we take off the prize.'

I went and fetched Swift Sam. 'He's small,' I said. 'But he's fast. I bet he can beat Murphy's mouse. It's called Mugger.'

We started to train Swift Sam. Every day after school we took him around a track in the back yard. We tied a piece of cheese on the end of a bit of string. Swift Sam chased after it as fast as he could. After six laps we gave him the piece of cheese to eat. At the start he could do six laps in ten minutes. By the end of the month he was down to three minutes.

'Scrag Murphy, look out,' said Pete with a grin. 'We are really going to beat the pants off you this time.'

The day of the big race came at last. There were about one hundred kids in Smith's barn. No adults knew about it – they would probably have stopped it if they knew. It cost fifty cents to get in. That's where the prize money came from. A kid called Tiger Gleeson took up the money and gave out the prize at the end. He was the organizer of the whole thing.

Scrag Murphy was there, of course, 'It's in the bag,' he swaggered. 'Mugger can't lose. I've fed him on a special diet. He is the fittest mouse in the county. He will eat Swift Sam, just you wait and see.'

I didn't say anything. But I was very keen to see his mouse, Mugger. Scrag Murphy had it in a box. No one had seen it yet.

'Right,' said Tiger. 'Get out your mice.' I put Swift Sam down on the track. He looked very small. He started sniffing around. I hoped he would run as fast with the other mice there – he hadn't had any match practice before. Then the others put their mice on the track. Everyone except Scrag Murphy. He still had Mugger in the box.

Scrag Murphy put his hand in the box and took out Mugger. He was the biggest mouse I had ever seen. He was at least ten times as big as Swift Sam. 'Hey,' said Pete. 'That's not a mouse. That's a rat. You can't race a rat. It's not fair.'

'It's not a rat,' said Scrag Murphy in a threatening voice. 'It's just a big mouse. I've been feeding it up'. I looked at it again. It was a rat all right. It was starting to attack the mice.

'We will take a vote,' said Tiger. 'All those that think it is a rat, put your hands up.' He counted all the hands.

'Fifty,' he said. 'Now all those who say that Mugger is a mouse put your hands up.' He counted again.

'Fifty-two. Mugger is a mouse.'

Scrag Murphy and his gang started to cheer. He had brought all his mates with him. It was a put-up job.

'Right,' said Tiger Gleeson. 'Get ready to race.'

There were about ten mice in the race – or I should say nine mice and one rat. Two rats if you counted Scrag Murphy. All the owners took out their string and cheese. 'Go,' shouted Tiger Gleeson.

Mugger jumped straight on to a little mouse next to him and bit it on the neck. The poor thing fell over and lay still. 'Boo,' yelled some of the crowd.

Swift Sam ran to the front straight away. He was going really well. Then Mugger started to catch up. It was neck and neck for five laps. First Mugger would get in front, then Swift Sam. Everyone in the barn went crazy. They were yelling their heads off.

By the sixth lap Mugger started to fall behind. All the other mice were not in the race. They had been lapped twice by Mugger and Swift Sam. But Mugger couldn't keep up with Swift Sam; he was about a tail behind. Suddenly something terrible happened. Mugger jumped onto Swift Sam's tail and grabbed it in his teeth. The crowd started to boo. Even Scrag Murphy's mates were booing.

But Swift Sam kept going. He didn't stop for a second. He just pulled that great rat along after him. It rolled over and over behind the little mouse. Mugger held on for grim death, but he couldn't stop Swift Sam. 'What a mouse,' screamed the crowd as Swift Sam crossed the finish line still towing Mugger behind him.

Scrag Murphy stormed off out of the barn. He didn't even take Mugger with him. Tiger handed me the fifty dollars. Then he held up Swift Sam. 'Swift Sam is the winner,' he said. 'The only mouse in the world with its own little pair of fairy underpants.'

Tama Gotcher
Robert Dawson

Tama Gotcher. Yes, that's what it was called. And it gotchered us all right. One minute we were a couple of mates wandering through the seaside arcades and sniffing our way past the stalls selling rock, chips, dough-nuts, burgers and what not. The next we had problems.

Sorry. I'm jumping ahead. There was me, of course, and my mate Bazzer with me. His mum and dad must have hated him when he was born by calling him Basil. I mean, I ask you. So since I first met him when I was a toddler and so was he, I called him Bazzer. I couldn't say Basil then. Just as well.

We were walking along the promenade near the sea. It was one of those fantastic seaside days when the sun's hot first thing in the morning. And boy, was it hot now, at noon!

Reaching one of the flights of steps down to the beach, we came across a man with a tray of things for sale. Bazzer's a sucker for that sort of thing. So we went to look.

He had a tray of tamagotchis. Big ones that you could clip on to your belt and walk round with. 'Tamagotchis. Get your tamagotchis here!' the man was calling.

He chewed gum like there was no tomorrow. So much so, that when he said 'Tamagotchi' it didn't quite sound right. Later, I realized he did it on purpose. Occasionally he gasped, as the lump of gum threatened to go down his throat and choke him. A sucker waiting for two suckers.

Later, also I wished it *had* blocked his airways.

'Here kids, just the thing for you,' he said. 'Your own tamagotchi. Feed it, clean it, train it, play with it – see it grow to old age and go to virtual heaven.'

'How much?' Bazzer askcd.

'Twenty quid,' he replied, and looked shiftier than ever.

'Twenty?' I nearly fainted. 'He must think we came here on the sucker boat!'

The salesman looked hurt. 'These ones talk. They're not like them in the shops!' He pushed one under our noses like a packet of gum.

'Hello!' said the Tama. Only what it really said was 'he-oh.'

'It's cute!' Bazzer took it. 'Hello!'

'He oh,' it answered. 'You fee me. You love me.'

'Hey, isn't it good! Hello little Tama.'

Before I could do anything to stop him, Bazzer had taken two tenners from his pocket and was holding them out to the man. Just then, a policeman came along, and the vendor snatched the notes and set off running in the opposite direction, gasping for air as he tried to chew.

'How much?' the policeman asked, and when Bazzer told him, he said, 'Mug!'

We sat down on the wall beside the prom to look more closely. We had a good start – there were no instructions. It was whilst we were searching the outside to find any sort of clues what to do that we found the maker's label. 'Tama gotcher. Made in China.'

'It isn't even a proper Japanese one,' said Bazzer. 'What's a Tama gotcher?'

'Ever been got?' I asked. 'For a tenner I'd have warned you not to buy it, only you never gave me a chance.'

'Fee me!' said the Tama, suddenly. It was so loud I jumped. We studied the creature on its little screen. It looked like a blob of jelly whose edges changed all the time. Like one of those amoebae they make you look at under a microscope in science, but with two eyes and a face.

'Fee me now!' it insisted.

'Turn the volume down!' I almost screamed.

Bazzer shook his head. 'There isn't one.'

We were just puzzling what to do when a series of little symbols appeared on the screen. One was a plate of food with a knife and fork, and the others were a glass with a straw sticking out, dustpan and brush, TV screen, ball, bed and revolver.

'What on earth's the gun for?' I asked.

'I don't know, but it's food it wants now.' He pressed the plate symbol. I found it difficult to imagine an armless creature eating with a knife and fork. Sorry, kny and for, I expect, in Tama gotcher speak.

After a slight pause, the Tama said, 'Long live the People's Republic of China.' A man walking past stared at the sound.

'Great,' I sighed. 'That's handy at the seaside.'

'You can't have everything!' Bazzer tried to reassure me.

It didn't work. 'You could still have twenty quid instead of a fake electronic game,' I countered.

'Yeah, well I wanted it. I like it. And it was my money.'

I couldn't argue with that. It was. And he'd worked hard on his paper round to get it. In all the worst weather of last winter.

We walked in silence for a few moments, then 'What shall we call it?' Bazzer asked. 'If you press this button on the side, it says, "Enter your Tama gotcher's name by speaking it".'

'"You're-a-mug", springs to mind,' I sighed. 'Or you could just call it Tama. You won't have it long enough to call it anything good.'

'I know, I could do like a Bazzer version of Tama, as it's mine, and call it "Tazzer".' And so it was.

I didn't bother to argue. It didn't seem worth it.

As we walked along, Bazzer kept gazing at the Tama and talking to it in a stupid baby way. 'Cootchy cootchy coo', and 'Hello little Tazzer!'

'Long live the People's Republic of China,' the wretched thing kept answering.

It asked for things all the time. I began to think it'd never shut up. 'Tazzer play', 'Tazzer watch telly', 'Tazzer sleep', only each time it didn't finish its words. It sounded even sillier when it wanted a drink – 'Tazzer sup', it said. It was beginning to get on my nerves.

'Can't you turn it down?' I asked. 'Everyone's staring.'

'Keeps you busy, doesn't it,' said Bazzer. 'Who's a naughty little Tazzer, then? Whoops, it needs cleaning again,' he said regretfully.

I knew what he meant. It seemed a lot of money to have spent on something which wanted your attention the whole time and did nothing back except repeat, 'Long live the People's Republic of China'. That made it worse. I began to resent the thing. I thought of the gun symbol and half wished it'd turn the gun on itself. The Tama-pain-in-the-neck, I mean.

We wandered through into some of the back streets to get into the shade and avoid some of the staring people.

Almost immediately I heard something. Shouting and some kind of action. I glanced over the road. There was a bank there, and that's where the commotion was coming from.

At first, I thought they were filming some kind of action scene for a soap or something. Then I realized this was no acting. A young man – not much older than us – came out of the bank waving a gun, and carrying a bag which must've contained money. Exactly like those action dramas you see on the telly.

The bank robber – I'd twigged by then – waved the gun in the air. He looked scared rigid. I understood how he felt. I ducked behind a parked car and watched through the side window. I'm no fool, and catching bullets isn't my favourite pastime. But Bazzer didn't. Well, that's typical of him.

Bazzer said later that he was so excited he just forgot to duck.

Then the Tama Gotcher intervened. 'Long live the People's Republic of China,' it said.

The man with the gun spun round as if we'd shot him in the back. His face was a picture. I could see his point, when you're in the middle of a robbery, it is a bit off-putting to have that called at you.

Bazzer said later it was the man swinging round which scared him most. So much so, he *still* didn't duck and weave.

The Tama Gotcher said, 'Tazzer sup!'

I didn't realize at the time why the man pointed the gun at us. Only later I thought how like 'Hands up!' the Tazzer's request for a drink must have sounded to an escaping and nervous bank robber.

The robber didn't escape. Instead, he put up his hands. But at that precise moment, when it looked like it was all over, Bazzer must have pressed the wrong button. He swears he pressed the drinks button, but he can't have. It must have been the gun symbol. There was a huge bang as the Tama's gun went off. The Tama gave a cry of anguish, and almost simultaneously Bazzer dropped it. The robber screamed and dropped the gun. If it'd've been me, so would I.

But *his* gun wasn't electronic.

Bazzer screamed as Tazzer crashed on the pavement and sort of exploded into lots of little bits of miniature transistors and plastic and solder. A lump of electronic toy flew in the air and crashed on the car roof. Bazzer fell over. (He wasn't hurt, just scared rigid. Later, he said he thought the bank robber had fired. But he hadn't, it wasn't even a real gun.)

The robber put his hands up even higher. He kept sobbing, 'They shot at me – those boys! And on my first bank job.'

It was then that I guessed he was on his bank robbery work experience.

It was also then that the police arrived.

Bazzer kept saying, 'He shot my Tama Gotcher! He shot my Tama Gotcher! How could he have shot my baby?'

'Oh shut up!' I growled, as we drove back to the guest house in the back of a police car. 'You pressed the wrong button. What a waste of money! Twenty quid for something that nearly got us killed. A Tama Gotcher all right!' I grumbled.

'It was my special pet,' Bazzer pouted. 'I loved it.'

'Yuk,' I answered. I heard the police driver snigger.

'How can you love an electronic . . . ' he began.

'Just don't ask,' I advised.

I don't know if it's true, but I've been told since that the gun symbol on the toy *is* for you to shoot the wretched thing when you get sick of it. I mean, when you feel it's deserved the chance to go to virtual heaven. Presumably it shot itself when Bazzer pressed the wrong button. And a good thing too.

The other good thing was the reward. Ten per cent of the money recovered.

Our bad luck was that the robber was only just learning his trade. All he'd snatched was four hundred pounds. Which was forty reward. Split two ways.

Still, at least Bazzer got his money back.

I gave mum my Christmas list the other day. I like to be in advance. And I'll give you one guess what's *not* on it.

The Dolls
Ian McEwan

Ever since he could remember, Peter had shared a
bedroom with Kate. Most of the time, he did not mind.
Kate was all right. She made him laugh. And there were
nights when Peter woke from a nightmare and was glad
to have someone else in the room, even if it was his
seven-year-old sister who would be no use against the
red-skinned, slime-covered creatures who chased him
through his sleep. When he woke up, these monsters
slid behind the curtains, or crept into the wardrobe.
Because Kate was in the room, it was just that little bit
easier to get out of bed and sprint across the landing to
his parents' room.

But there were times when he did mind sharing a
room. And Kate minded too. There were long afternoons
when they got on each other's nerves. A squabble would
lead to a row, and a row to a fight, a proper punching,
scratching, hair-pulling fight. Since Peter was three
years older he expected to win these all-out battles. And
in a sense, he did. He could always count on making Kate
cry first.

But was this really winning? Kate could hold her breath
and push and make her face the colour of a ripe plum. All
she needed to do then was run downstairs and show her
mother 'what Peter did'. Or she might lie on the floor
making a rattling sound in her throat so that Peter
thought she was about to die. Then *he* would have to run
down the stairs to fetch his mother. Kate could also
scream. Once, during one of her noise storms, a car
passing the house had stopped and a worried man had
got out and stared up at the bedroom window. Peter was

looking out at the time. The man ran up the garden and hammered on the door, certain something terrible was happening inside. And it was. Peter had borrowed something of Kate's, and she wanted it back. *Now*!

On these occasions, Peter was the one who got into trouble, and Kate was the one who came out on top. This was how Peter saw it. When he got angry with Kate, he had to think carefully before hitting her. Often they kept the peace by drawing an imaginary line from the door right across their bedroom. Kate's side there, Peter's side here. On this side, Peter's drawing and painting table, his one soft toy, a giraffe with a bent neck, the chemistry and electricity and printing sets that were never as much fun as the pictures on the box lids promised, and the tin trunk he kept his secrets in, which Kate was always trying to open.

Over there were Kate's painting and drawing table, her telescope, microscope and magnetism sets which *were* as much fun as the pictures on their lids promised, and everywhere else in her half of the room were the dolls. They sat along the window-ledge with their legs dangling idly, they balanced on her chest of drawers and flopped over its mirror, they sat in a toy pram, jammed like tube-train commuters. The ones in favour crept nearer her bed. They were all colours, from shiny boot-polish black to deathly white, though most were a glowing pink. Some were naked. Others wore only one item, a sock, a T-shirt, or a bonnet. A few were dressed to the nines in ball-gowns with sashes, lace-trimmed frocks, and long skirts trailing ribbons. They were all quite different, but they all had one thing in common: they all had the same wide, mad, unblinking angry stare. They were meant to be babies, but their eyes gave them away. Babies never looked at anyone like that. When he walked past the dolls, Peter felt watched, and when he was out of the room, he suspected they were talking about him, all sixty of them.

Still, they never did Peter any harm, and there was only one that he really disliked. The Bad Doll. Even Kate did not like it. She was scared of it, so scared she did not dare throw it out in case it came back in the middle of the night and took its revenge. You would know the Bad Doll at a glance. It was a pink that no human had ever been. Long ago, its left leg and right arm had been wrenched from their sockets, and from the top of its pitted skull grew one thick hank of black hair. Its makers had wanted to give it a sweet little smile, but something must have gone wrong with the mould because the Bad Doll always curled its lips in scorn, and frowned, as if trying to remember the nastiest thing in the world.

Of all the dolls, only the Bad Doll was neither boy nor girl. The Bad Doll was simply 'it'. It was naked, and sat as far as possible from Kate's bed, on a bookcase from where it looked down on the others. Kate sometimes took it in her hands and tried to soothe it with her murmurs, but it was never long before she shuddered and quickly put it back.

The invisible line worked well when they remembered about it. They had to ask permission to cross to the other's half. Kate was not to pry into Peter's secret trunk, and Peter was not to touch Kate's microscope without asking. It worked well enough until one wet Sunday afternoon they had a row, one of their worst, about where exactly this line was. Peter was sure it was further away from his bed. This time, Kate did not need to turn purple or pretend to die, or scream. She clocked Peter on the nose with the Bad Doll. She held it by its one fat pink leg and swung it at his face. So it was Peter who went running downstairs crying. His nose was not actually hurting, but it was bleeding, and he wanted to make the most of it.

As he hurried down, he smeared blood over his face with the back of his hand, and when he came into the kitchen, he dropped to the floor in front of his mother and wailed and moaned and writhed. Sure enough, Kate got into trouble, big trouble.

This was the fight that led their parents to decide that it was time Peter and Kate had separate rooms. Not long after Peter's tenth birthday, his father cleared out what was called the 'box room', even though it contained no boxes, only old picture frames and broken armchairs. Peter helped his mother decorate the room. They hung curtains and squeezed in a huge iron bed with brass knobs on.

Kate was so happy she helped Peter carry his stuff across the landing. No more fights. And she would no longer have to listen to the disgusting gurgling, piping noise her brother made in his sleep. And Peter could not stop singing. Now he had a place where he could go and, well, just *be*. That night he chose to go to bed half an hour early in order to enjoy his own place, his own things, with no imaginary line down the middle of the room. He lay in the semi-darkness and thought that it was just as well that some good at last had come from that vile monstrosity, the Bad Doll.

So the months passed, and Peter and Kate became used to having their own rooms and no longer gave it much thought. The interesting dates came and went – Peter's birthday, firework night, Christmas, Kate's birthday, and then Easter. It was two days after the family Easter egg hunt. Peter was in his room, on his bed, about to eat his last egg. It was the biggest, the heaviest, which was why he had saved it until last. He peeled off the silver and blue foil wrapper. It was almost the size of a rugby ball. He held it in two hands, gazing at it. Then he drew it towards him and pushed into the shell with his thumbs.

How he loved the thick, buttery cocoa aroma that poured
from the dark hollowness inside. He raised the egg to his
nose and breathed in. Then he started to eat.

Outside, it was raining. There was still a week of
holidays. Kate was out at a friend's house. There was
nothing to do but eat. Twenty minutes later, all that was
left of the egg was the wrapper. Peter got to his feet,
swaying slightly. He felt sick and bored, a perfect
combination for a wet afternoon. How strange it was,
having his own room was not exciting any more. 'Sick of
chocolate,' he sighed as he went towards his door. 'Sick
of my room!'

He stood on the landing, wondering if he was about to
be sick. But instead of heading to the lavatory, he walked
towards Kate's room and stepped inside. He had been
back hundreds of times before, of course, but never
alone. He stood in the centre of the room, watched, as
usual, by the dolls. He felt peculiar, and everything
looked different. The room was bigger, and he had never
noticed before how the floor sloped. There seemed to
be more dolls than ever with their glassy stares, and as he
went down the slope towards his old bed, he thought
he heard a sound, a rustling. He thought he saw something move, but when he turned, everything was still.

He sat on the bed and thought back over the old days
when he had slept here. He'd been just a kid then. Nine!
What could he have known? If only his ten-year-old self
could go back and tell that innocent fool what was
what. When you got to ten, you began to see the whole
picture, how things connected, how things worked . . .
an overview . . .

Peter was so intent on trying to remember his ignorant
younger self of six months before that he did not notice
the figure making its way across the carpet towards him.
When he did, he gave out a shout of surprise and

scrambled right on to the bed, and drew his knees up. Coming towards him at an awkward but steady pace was the Bad Doll. It had taken a paintbrush from Kate's desk to use as a crutch. It hobbled across the room with bad-tempered gasps, and it was muttering swear words that even a bad doll should not use. It stopped by the bedpost to get its breath. Peter was surprised to notice how sweaty its forehead and upper lip were. The Bad Doll leaned the paintbrush against the bed and drew its only forearm across its face. And then, with a quick glance at Peter, and taking a deep breath, the Bad Doll snatched up its crutch and set about climbing on to the bed.

Scrambling up three times your own height with only one arm and a leg takes patience and strength. The Bad Doll had little of either. Its little pink body quivered with the effort and strain as it hung half-way up the post, looking for leverage for its paintbrush. The gasps and grunts became louder and more piteous. Slowly the head, sweatier than ever, rose into Peter's view. He could easily have reached over and lifted the creature on to the bed. And just as easily, he could have swatted it to the floor. But he did nothing. It was all too interesting. He wanted to see what happened. As the Bad Doll inched its way up with cries of 'Oh blast and hell's teeth!' and 'Damnation take the grit!' and 'Filthy custard!' Peter became aware that the head of every doll in the room was turned in his direction. Pure blue eyes blazed wider than ever, and there was a soft whispering of sibilants like water tumbling over rocks, a sound which gathered into a murmur, and then a torrent as excitement swept through five dozen spectators.

'He's doing it!' Peter heard one of them call.

And another answered, 'Now we'll see something!'

And yet another called out, 'What's fair is fair!' and at least twenty dolls shouted their agreement.

'Yes!'

'That's right!'

'Well put!'

The Bad Doll had got its arm on to the bed and had let go of its crutch. Now it was clawing at the blanket, trying to get a grip so it could pull itself up. And even as it was doing this, on the other side of the room there arose an almighty cheer, and suddenly the dolls, all the dolls, were making their way towards the bed. From window-sills and from on top of the mirror, from Kate's bed and from out of the toy pram, they came springing and leaping, spilling and tumbling and surging across the carpet. Dolls in long dresses shrieked as they stumbled and tripped, while naked dolls, or one-sock dolls, moved with horrible ease. On they came, a wave of brown and pink and black and white, and on every moulded pouting lip was the cry 'What's fair is fair! What's fair is fair!' And in every wide glassy eye was the anger that Peter had always suspected behind the pretty baby blue.

The Bad Doll had made it on to the bed and was standing, exhausted but proud, waving to the crowd gathered below. The dolls pressed tight together and roared their approval, and raised their chubby, dimpled arms towards their leader.

'What's fair is fair!' the chant began again.

Peter had moved down to the far end of the bed. His back was to the wall and his arms were clasped round his knees. This really was extraordinary. Surely his mother would hear the racket downstairs and come up to tell them to be quiet.

The Bad Doll needed to catch its breath, so it was letting the chant go on. Then it picked up the paintbrush crutch and the dolly rabble was suddenly silent.

With a wink for the benefit of its supporters, the lame doll hopped a pace or two closer to Peter and said,

'Settled in nicely, have you?' Its tone was very polite, but there were titters in the crowd, and Peter knew he was being set up.

'I'm not sure what you mean,' he said.

The Bad Doll turned to the crowd and did a good imitation of Peter's voice. 'He's not sure what I mean.' It turned back to Peter. 'I mean, comfortable in your new room, are you?'

'Oh that,' Peter said. 'Yes, my room is terrific.'

Some of the dolls down on the carpet seized on this word and repeated it over and over again, 'Terrific . . . terrific . . . terrific . . .' until it began to sound like a very stupid word indeed, and Peter wished he had not used it.

The Bad Doll waited patiently. When all was quiet again it asked, 'Like having your own room, do you?'

'I do,' Peter replied.

'Like having a room all to yourself?'

'Yes. I just told you. I like it,' Peter said.

The Bad Doll hobbled one pace closer. Peter had the feeling that it was about to come to the point. It raised its voice. 'And have you ever considered that someone else might want that room?'

'That's ridiculous,' Peter said. 'Mum and Dad share a room. That leaves only Kate and me . . .'

His words were drowned out by a roar of disapproval from the crowd. The Bad Doll managed to balance on one leg while it raised its crutch in the air for silence.

'Only two of you, eh?' it said, nodding towards the crowd.

Peter laughed. He couldn't think of what to say.

The Bad Doll came even closer. Peter could have reached out and touched it. He was sure he could smell chocolate on its breath.

'Don't you think,' it said, 'that it's time someone else had a turn in that room?'

'That's ridiculous,' Peter started to say. 'You're only dolls . . .'

Nothing could have made the Bad Doll more furious. 'You've seen how we live,' it screamed. 'Sixty of us squashed into one corner of the room. You've passed us a thousand times, and you've never given it a thought. What do you care that we're piled on top of each other like bricks in a wall. You just don't see what's in front of you. Look at us! No space, no privacy, not even a bed for most of us. Now it's someone else's turn with that room. What's fair is fair!'

Another great roar went up from the crowd, and once again, the chant was taken up. 'What's fair is fair! What's fair is fair!' And as it was bellowed out, the dolls began to swarm up on to the bed, standing on each other's shoulders to make ladders of their bodies. Within a minute, the whole crew stood panting before Peter, and the Bad Doll, who had retreated to the far end of the bed, waved its crutch from the back of the crowd and shouted, 'Now!'

Sixty pairs of chubby hands took hold of Peter's left leg.

'Yo-ho heave-ho!' sang out the Bad Doll.

'Yo-ho heave-ho!' answered the crowd.

And then a strange thing happened. Peter's leg came off. It came right off. He looked down at where his leg used to be, and instead of blood there was a little coiled spring poking out through his torn trousers.

That's funny, he thought. I never would have guessed . . .

But he did not have much time to think about how funny it was because now the dolls had grabbed his right arm and were pulling and yo-ho heave-ho-ing, and his arm was off too, and sticking out from his shoulder was another little spring.

'Hey!' Peter shouted. 'Give those back.'

But it was no use. The arm and leg were being passed over the heads in the crowd, back towards the Bad Doll. It took the leg and slotted it on. A perfect fit. Now it was putting the arm in place. That arm could have been made specially, it fitted so well.

Odd, Peter thought. I'm sure my arm and leg would be too big.

Even as he was thinking this, the dolls were on him again, and this time they were scrambling up his chest, pulling his hair, ripping at this clothes.

'Get off,' Peter shouted. 'Ouch! That hurts.'

The dolls laughed as they yanked out nearly all his hair. They left one long hank sticking out of the middle of his head.

The Bad Doll tossed Peter its crutch, and leaped up and down to test its new leg. 'My turn for that room,' it called. 'And as for him, he can go up there.' It pointed with what Peter still thought of as *his* arm at the bookcase. The Bad Doll leaped nimbly to the floor, and the crowd swept forwards to seize Peter and carry him off to his new home. And that is how it would have ended. But just then, Kate stepped into the room.

Now, you have to try and imagine the scene from where she stood. She had come home from playing with her friend, she had walked into her bedroom, and there was her brother, lying on the spare bed, playing with her dolls, *all* her dolls, and he was moving them around, and doing their voices. The only one not on the bed was the Bad Doll, which was lying on the carpet nearby.

Kate could have got angry. After all, this was against the rules. Peter was in her room without her permission, *and* he had taken down all her dolls from their special places. But instead, Kate laughed to see her brother with sixty dolls piled on top of him.

Peter stood up quickly as soon as he saw Kate. He was blushing.

'Oh . . . er . . . sorry,' he mumbled, and he tried to edge past her.

'Wait a minute,' Kate said. 'What about putting this lot back. They all have their own places, you know.'

So, while Kate told him where they belonged, Peter put every single doll back in its place, on the mirror, the chest of drawers, the window-sills, the bed, the pram.

It seemed to take for ever to get them all in place. The very last to be returned was the Bad Doll. As Peter set it down on top of the bookcase, he was sure he heard it say, 'One day, my friend, that room will be mine.'

'Oh, damnation take the grit!' Peter whispered to it. 'You filthy mustard!'

'What did you say?' Kate called out. But her brother had already stepped out of the room.

A Prawn in the Game
Elaine Sishton

I was doing some homework in the lounge and mum was cleaning the curtain rail when dad came in. She left it to pour him a drink. He grunted 'hello', took the glass from her and slumped into the nearest chair. He didn't look at me at all, but then again, he never did.

'Had a good day?' mum asked cheerfully, 'I've got your favourite. Prawn cocktail and a nice steak.'

He glared at her.

'What's the matter?' she asked. I looked up at him. Another argument was coming.

"I'm leaving you, Elizabeth,' he said coldly.

A flicker of a nervous smile crossed mum's face. I stood up and looked quickly from one to the other. Mum opened her mouth as if to speak but nothing came out. I stared at him, waiting. He spoke into the bottom of his glass first of all, then directly, he looked up. 'What I really mean is, you're both leaving me. The house is in my name – always has been, and I want Julia to move in with me.'

'Julia?' mum echoed.

'Yes, Julia. The woman I adore.' His voice was raised now. Mum grabbed the back of the chair to steady herself and I noticed that her knuckles had turned white.

'But . . . I thought we were happy . . . ' her voice trailed off.

'Happy!' he scoffed. 'How could anyone be happy with you? I've only stayed married to you for so long because I felt sorry for you.'

'What do you mean?'

'You're a simpering fool! No mind of your own. That's what I mean. To top it all, that pathetic excuse for a son is just like you. You're both idiots!'

'It's not Mark's fault,' mum said, putting her hands on my shoulders. 'Have you thought about *him*?'

'What about him? You've namby-pambied him since he was born.'

'But he needs us both.'

'For God's sake, woman. He's thirteen years old!'

He was pointing at me and his words stabbed through my heart as surely as if he'd used a knife. I turned to mum. The tears streamed down her face, but she didn't say anything.

He stood up to face us.

'I'm staying with Julia tonight. We'll be back tomorrow afternoon. By then I want you and your things to have gone – I want both of you out of this house and out of my life.'

'Where will we go?' I asked mum. He leapt towards me, his hand raised. Mum pulled me behind her quickly.

'No, George. Not this time,' she hissed. He stopped, startled. It was the first time that mum had dared to face up to him. Slowly, he lowered his hand.

'Oh, for God's sake, go to your mother's. She only lives streets away. But get out of this house. Do you understand? I don't ever want you back.' He glared fiercely at her. She nodded. Then he walked out and was gone.

And that was that. My dad had left us.

Mum pulled herself round to the front of the chair and lowered herself into it gently. She perched on the edge, white-faced.

'Are you OK, mum?' I asked.

'I saw this coming,' she said, 'I guessed about a year ago that your dad was seeing another woman, but this wasn't the first time. I thought that he'd get over her, like all the rest.'

She started to cry and, although I tried not to, so did I. We held each other for a while, then she got up and put on her coat.

'Come on, we'll go to Nan's. We'll come back in the morning for our things,' she said.

'Why? Why do we have to go? This is our home, too,' I sniffed.

'Your dad is quite right. Everything is in his name, love. Come on, now.' She picked up her handbag, and we walked into the kitchen. Mum turned off the cooker and we left.

Nan was surprised to see us. We sat in the living room, in front of a roaring fire, drinking tea and eating warm buttered toast. Mum did her best to explain what had happened. At last Nan tutted crossly.

'This is your own fault, Elizabeth. For most of your life I've been telling you to stand up for yourself. What do you think your father would have said about all this? What about Mark?' Nan looked over at me. 'He's a smashing lad. How can George not love him?'

'He does love him, mother,' mum said, wide-eyed. But I knew she was lying.

'You know we never really liked George. Your father thought he was a bully and a nasty piece of work.'

'Did he?' mum said sadly. 'You never said.'

'It wasn't for us to interfere. But for goodness sake stand up for yourself now. Do it for Mark and me and your father, if no one else. He's going to take everything from you – your home, your possessions and a good chunk of your life. Are you just going to sit back and let him?'

'Everything is in his name, mother, I have no choice.'

'That's not true. You know you're entitled to half. Fight back, Elizabeth. Don't let him get away with this. He needs to be taught a lesson.'

'I'm going to bed.' Mum got up slowly. She kissed me and then Nan, on the cheek, and made her way upstairs. Nan watched her go, shaking her head sadly.

'Come on, Mark,' she smiled and hugged me. 'Everything's going to be all right.'

I lay in bed for a long time, thinking. Nan was right of course, dad had treated both me and mum badly over the years. He'd never once sent either of us a birthday card, or given presents. We'd never been on holiday together, either. Dad was always off on business trips. Then there were terrible times when he would hit both of us. I'd have to have days off school until the bruises went, and mum had twice been to the hospital for her 'little accidents'. She was afraid to tell anyone it was dad. So was I.

Thoughts ran endlessly around my head. Deep down I knew, though, that dad needed to be taught a lesson.

The next morning, as we drove home, mum said, 'I'm going to stand up for us this time, Mark.' So, she'd been doing some thinking too. Once home, mum wrote dad a note and left it where he was sure to see it. I read it through. It explained that she was going to see a solicitor and that she wanted a divorce and half of everything. Mum said that she felt better once she'd written it. I looked around our home. Mum hadn't had time to replace the curtain rail she'd been cleaning. Another woman would be here tomorrow sitting on our chairs, cooking with our pans, drinking from our glasses! I felt so angry. I walked through to the kitchen and stood looking at the food that should have been dad's dinner last night. A defrosted packet of prawns lay on the side unit. I picked them up to put them in the fridge for mum. Then I stopped. A crazy idea crossed my mind.

I calmly walked into the lounge, opening the packet of prawns with my teeth. I lifted one side of the brass curtain rail and pulled off the end. Carefully I began emptying the prawns into the hollow rail. Mum came in just then.

'What on earth are you doing?' she asked, looking at the prawn packet in one hand and the curtain rail in the other.

'Sshh!' I motioned. She looked puzzled for a moment, then she began to giggle.

'We can't!' she said, coming over to help. I poured in the rest of the packet then we gave the rail a final bump to distribute the prawns as evenly as possible. Mum put the end of the rail back and we lifted the whole thing on to its brackets.

We collected all our stuff, loaded it into the car and left.

'I can't believe what we've just done,' mum kept saying.

Nan couldn't either!

It was two weeks later that mum got a telephone call from dad. He asked if he could meet her at a coffee-house nearby. He sounded very cross. I asked to go with her. After all, if he'd found out about the prawns business, it had been my idea. When we arrived he was already waiting. He glanced up as we got to the table and frowned. We sat down.

'What's he doing here?' he nodded his head in my direction.

'This is your son,' mum tutted.

'You're late!' He fidgeted about with a paper napkin on the table. 'I never thought you'd do this to me, Elizabeth.'

'Do what?' she asked, startled.

'Ruin me.'

'Well, I'm entitled to my share of our years together, you know. You weren't the easiest of men to live with. By the way, thank you for asking, we're both fine. How are you and Julia?'

He looked at her properly for the first time.

'We're moving out of that house,' he said. 'You can move back if you want and give me half the worth of the place.'

My heart jumped into my mouth. I'd enjoyed staying at Nan's, but a chance to go home was brilliant.

'Well, I'll certainly think it over. Is everything all right, George? You seem worried.'

'You may as well know,' he sighed crossly. 'We've had to have workmen out. There's an awful stink from somewhere.'

'A smell?' mum raised her eyebrows. 'There was no smell when we lived there.' She grabbed my hand under the table and we squeezed for all we were worth.

'Well, there is now. A terrible stink.'

'Did they find anything? The workmen?' mum asked in mock concern.

'Not a thing. It's an awful rotting smell – I've never known anything like it. I think it must be a break in a sewer pipe.'

'Dear me. I am sorry.' Mum leaned across the table and patted his hand. He pulled away quickly.

'Are you?' he glared.

The waiter came then and mum ordered a coffee for herself and a glass of orange for me. As she was finishing her cup, mum said, 'You know, George, we *will* move back in. We'll have the house valued and give you and Julia half.'

'You'll give me half. Julia has nothing to do with it!'

'Well, *you* then. Let me know when we can move back.'

'This weekend. We're moving to Julia's old flat.'

'Flat?' Mum sounded shocked.

'Move back this weekend. I'll be glad to see the back of the place, and that damn awful smell.'

I took a big gulp of orange as he pushed back his chair and left.

'Goodbye, George', smiled mum, when he'd gone.

'Bye, dad,' I said, and suddenly felt very sorry for Julia.

So the following Saturday there we were, sitting in the middle of our empty lounge. They'd taken almost everything with them. We somehow knew this was a new start for both of us and strangely enough we looked forward to it. Mum was stronger now and not so afraid.

We looked at each other and at the same time we both looked up above the window. We laughed loudly. Nan came in.

'What are you two laughing about?' she smiled, putting her arms around our shoulders.

Then she followed our gaze and began laughing with us. It was perfect.

Dad and Julia had taken the brass curtain rail with them . . .

QWERTYUIOP
Vivien Alcock

Jobs don't grow on trees, the principal of the Belmont Secretarial College was fond of saying.

'Be positive,' Mrs Price told her departing students, as she shook them by the hand in turn. 'Go out into the world and *win*! I have every confidence in you.'

When she came to the last student, however, her confidence suddenly evaporated. She looked at Lucy Beck, and sighed.

'Good luck, my dear,' she said kindly, but rather in the tone of voice of someone wishing a snowman a happy summer.

Lucy Beck was young and small and mouse-coloured, easily overlooked. She had a lonely 'O' level and a typing speed that would make a tortoise laugh.

'Whoever will want to employ me?' she had asked Mrs Price once, and Mrs Price had been at a loss to answer.

Lucy wanted a job. More than anyone, more than anything, she wanted a job. She was tired of being poor. She was fed up with macaroni cheese and baked beans. She was sick of second-hand clothes.

'We are jumble sailors on the rough sea of life,' her mother would say.

Lucy loved her mother, but could not help wishing she would sometimes lose her temper. Shout. Scream. Throw saucepans at the spinning, grinning head of Uncle Bert.

If I get a job, I'm getting out. He's not drinking up my pay packet, that's for sure. *If* I get a job . . . Trouble was that there were hundreds after every vacancy, brighter than Lucy, better qualified than Lucy, wearing strings of 'O' levels round their necks like pearls.

Who in their right minds will choose me? Lucy wondered, setting off for her first interview.

So she was astonished to be greeted by Mr Ross, of Ross and Bannister's, with enormous enthusiasm. She was smiled at, shaken by the hand, given tea and biscuits, and told that her single 'O' level was the very one they had been looking for. Then she was offered the job.

'I hope you will be happy here,' Mr Ross said, showing her out. There was a sudden doubt in his voice, a hint of anxiety behind his smile, but she was too excited to notice.

'I've got the job! I've got the job!' she cried, running into the kitchen at home. 'I'm to start on Monday. I'm to be paid on Friday.'

Her mother turned to stare at her.

'You never! Fancy that now! Who'd have thought it!' she said in astonishment.

Lucy was not offended by her mother's surprise. She shared it. They never trusted luck, but looked at it suspiciously, as if at a stranger coming late to their door.

Ross and Bannister's was a small firm, with a factory just outside the town, making cushions and duvets; and an office in the High Street. On Monday morning, at ten to nine, the door to this office was shut and locked.

She was early. She smoothed down her windy hair, and waited.

At five past nine, an elderly man, with small dark eyes like currants and a thick icing of white hair, came hobbling up the stairs. He was jingling a bunch of keys.

'Ah,' he said, noticing Lucy. 'Punctuality is the courtesy of kings, – but a hard necessity for new brooms, eh? You *are* the new broom, I suppose? Not an impatient customer waiting to see our new range of sunburst cushions, by any chance?'

'I'm Lucy Beck,' she said, adding proudly, 'the new secretary.'

'Let's hope you stay longer than the other ones,' the man said, and unlocked the door. 'Come in, come in, Miss Beck. Come into the parlour, said the spider to the fly. I'm Harry Darke, thirty years with Ross and Bannister's, retired with a silver watch, and now come back to haunt the place. Can't keep away, you see.' Then he added oddly, half under his breath, 'Like someone else I could mention, but won't.'

He looked at Lucy, standing shy and awkward, clutching her bag and uncertain what to do. 'Poor Miss Beck, you mustn't mind old Harry. Part-time messenger, office boy, tea-maker, mender of fuses. Anything you want, just ask old Harry. Mr Ross is down at the factory in the morning, but he's left you plenty of work to be getting on with.' He pointed to a pile of tapes on the desk. 'Letters to be typed, those are. He got behindhand, with the last girl leaving so quick. Left the same day she came. Shot off like a scalded cat!'

'Why?' Lucy asked curiously.

'Hang your coat in the cupboard here,' he said, ignoring her question. 'Washroom along the passage to the right. Kitchenette to the left. We share it with Lurke and Dare, House Agents, and Mark Tower, Solicitor. No gossiping over the teapots, mind. Most of the young things go to Tom's Café for lunch. Put this sign on the door when you leave.' He handed her a cardboard notice on a looped string, on which was printed: Gone For Lunch. Back At Two. 'Now is there anything else you want to know before I slope off?'

'You're going?' Lucy asked, surprised.

'Yes, my girl. I've errands to do. Not frightened of holding the fort on your own, are you?'

'No, but . . .'

'You can take a telephone message without getting the names muddled, can't you?'

'Yes, of course.'

'Nothing else to it, is there? No need to look like a frightened mouse.'

'I'm *not*!'

He looked at her for a long moment, with a strange expression on his face, almost as if he were sorry for her.

'You're very young,' he said at last.

'I'm seventeen.'

'Don't look it. Look as if you should be still at school. This your first job?'

'Yes.'

He shook his head slowly, still regarding her with that odd pity.

'It's a shame,' he said; then, seeing her puzzled face, added briskly, 'Well, I'll be off then. Mr Ross will be in this afternoon.'

Yet still he stood there, looking at her. Embarrassed, Lucy turned away and took the cover off the typewriter.

'Just one last thing,' the old man said, 'that's an electric typewriter.'

'I'm used to electric typewriters,' Lucy said coldly. She was beginning to be annoyed.

'Not this one. This one's . . . different. You mustn't worry,' he said gently, 'if it goes a little wrong now and again. Just ignore it. Don't bother to re-type the letters. Splash on the old correcting fluid. Look, I got you a big bottle. Liquid Paper, the things they invent! And if that runs out, cross out the mistakes with a black pen – see, I've put one in your tray. Nice and thick it is. That should keep her quiet.'

'I don't make mistakes,' Lucy said; then honesty compelled her to add, 'well, not very many. I've been trained. I've got a diploma.'

'Yes. Yes, my dear, so they all had,' he said sadly, and left.

After the first moments of strangeness, Lucy was glad to be alone. No one breathing down her neck. She looked round the office with pleasure. Hers.

Sunlight streamed through the window. The curtains shifted a little in the spring breeze. There was a small blue and green rug on the floor.

I'll have daffodils in a blue vase, Lucy thought. I can afford flowers now. Or I will be able to, on Friday.

Better get on with the work. She sat down, switched on the typewriter, inserted paper and carbons, and started the first tape.

'Take a letter to Messrs. Black and Hawkins, 28, Market Street, Cardington. Dear Sirs . . . ' Mr Ross's voice came clearly and slowly out of the tape deck. Lucy began to type.

She was a touch-typist. She did not need to look at the keys. Her fingers kept up their slow, steady rhythm, while her eyes dreamed round the office, out of the window, down into the sunny street.

'. . . our new line of sunburst cushions in yellow, orange and pink,' came Mr Ross's voice.

There was something odd! A sudden wrongness felt by her fingers, a tingling, an icy pricking . . .

She snatched her fingers away and stared at the typewriter. It hummed back at her innocently. What was wrong? There was something . . . Her glance fell on the uncompleted letter.

Dear Sirs,
I am pleased to inform you that QWERTYUIOP and Bannister's have introduced a new QWERTYUIOP of sunburst cushions in QWERTYUIOP, orange and QWERTYUIOP . . .

She stared at it in horrified bewilderment. What had happened? What had she done? Not even on her first day at the Belmont Secretarial College had she made such ridiculous mistakes. Such strange mistakes – QWERTYUIOP, the top line of letters on a type-writer, repeated over and over again! Thank God there had been no one to notice. They'd think she had gone mad.

She must be more careful. Keep her mind on the job, not allow it to wander out of the window into the sunny shopping street below. Putting fresh paper into the typewriter, she began again.

She was tempted to look at the keyboard . . . 'Don't look at the keys! Keep your eyes away!' Mrs Price was always saying. 'No peeping. You'll never make a good typist if you can't do it by touch. Rhythm, it's all rhythm. Play it to music in your head.'

So Lucy obediently looked away, and typed to a slow tune in her head, dum diddle dum dee, dum diddle dum dee . . . Why did her fingers feel funny? Why were goosepimples shivering her flesh? Was the typewriter really humming *in tune*?

She sat back, clasping her hands together, and stared at the letter in the machine. It read:

Dear Sirs,
YOU ARE SITTING IN MY CHAIR to inform you that GO AWAY a new line of WE DO NOT WANT YOU HERE cushions in yellow, SILLY CHIT and pink. QWERTYUIOP.

She could not believe her eyes. She stared at the extraordinary words and trembled.

'Let's hope you stay longer than the other ones,' the old man had said.

Tears came into Lucy's eyes. She tore the sheets out of the typewriter and threw them into the wastepaper basket. Then she put in fresh paper and began again. Grimly, in defiance of Mrs Price's teaching, she kept her eyes fixed on the keyboard.

Dear Sirs,
We are pleased to inform you that Ross and Bannister's have introduced a new line of Sunburst cushions . . .

With a rattle the typewriter took over. She felt the keys hitting her fingers from below, leaping up and down like mad children at playtime. She took her hands away and watched.

. . . YOU CAN'T KEEP ME OUT THAT WAY, the typewriter printed. YOU'LL NEVER BE RID OF ME. NEVER. WHY DON'T YOU GO. NO ONE WANTS YOU HERE. NO ONE LIKES YOU. GO AWAY BEFORE

Then it stopped, its threat uncompleted.

Lucy leaped up overturning her chair and ran to the door.

'Left the same day she came,' the old man had said. 'Shot off like a scalded cat!'

'No!' Lucy shouted.

She left the door and went over to the window, looking down at the bright shops. She thought of jumble sales and baked beans. She thought of pretty new clothes and rump steaks. She might be young and shy and a little slow, but she was not, no, she was *not* a coward!

She went back and sat down in front of the typewriter and glared at it. There it crouched, like a squat, ugly monster, staring at her with its alphabetical eyes.

Lucy typed quickly:

Are you from outer space?

The typewriter rocked, as if with laughter, its keys clicking like badly fitting false teeth.

IDIOT, it wrote.

Who are you? Lucy typed.

MISS BROOME, it answered.

Lucy hesitated. She did not know quite how to reply to this. In the end she typed:

How do you do? I am Miss Beck.

GO AWAY, MISS BECK

Why should I?

I AM SECRETARY HERE, it stated, this time in red letters.

No, you're not! *I* am! Lucy typed angrily.

The machine went mad.

QUERTYUIOP!"/@QUERTYUIOP£-&()*QWERTY UIOP+!, it screamed, shaking and snapping its keys like castanets.

Lucy switched it off. She sat for a long time, staring in front of her, her face stubborn. Then she took the cap off the bottle of correcting fluid.

For an hour, she battled with the machine. As fast as QUERTYUIOPs and unwanted capitals appeared, she attacked with a loaded brush. The white fluid ran down the typing paper like melting ice-cream, and dripped thickly into the depths of the typewriter.

YOU'RE DROWNING ME, it complained pathetically, and she swiped at the words with her brush.

HELP!

Another swipe.

PLEASE!

But Lucy showed no mercy. The large bottle was half-empty when she reached the end of the letter in triumph.

Yours faithfully,

George Ross,

she typed, and sat back with a sigh of relief.

The machine began to rattle. Too late, Lucy snatched the completed letter out of the typewriter. Across the bottom of the otherwise faultless page, it now said in large, red capitals:

I HATE YOU!

Furiously she painted the words out.

Mr Ross came to the office at four o'clock. His eyes went to the corner of the desk where Lucy had put the completed letters. If he was surprised to find so modest a number after a day's work, he did not say so, but picked them up.

'Any telephone messages?' he asked.

'On your desk, sir,' Lucy said and went to make him tea.

When she brought it in on a flowered metal tray, she found Mr Ross signing the last letter, his pen skidding awkwardly over the thick shiny layer of plastic paper. All the letters were heavily damasked with the dried fluid, like starched table napkins. He glanced up at her a little unhappily.

'Did you have trouble with the machine, Miss Beck?' he asked.

'Yes, sir.' (She was afraid to say what trouble in case he thought she was mad.)

'It's only just come back from being serviced,' he said wearily.

'I'm sorry, sir. It keeps . . . going wrong.'

There was a long silence. Then he said with a sigh, 'I see. Well, do what you can. If it's no better at the end of the week . . .'

He let the sentence hang in the air, so that she was not certain whether it would be the typewriter or Lucy Beck who would get the chop.

The next morning, Harry Darke raised his eyebrows when he saw Lucy.

'Still here?' he exclaimed. 'Well done, my dear. I never thought I'd be seeing you again. You're braver than you look. Fighting back, eh?'

'Yes,' said Lucy briefly. She walked past him and went up to the desk. *Her* desk. Then she took out of her carrier bag a small bunch of daffodils and a blue vase.

'Staking your claim, I see,' the old man said, regarding her with admiration. 'D'you want me to fill that for you?'

'Thanks.'

He came back, carrying a tray.

'Thought I might as well make us tea while I was about it,' he said. 'Here's your vase.'

'Thanks.'

'I'll be here till one o'clock today,' he said, as she arranged her flowers. 'Anything you want to know? Any snags come up I can help you with? Light bulbs changed. Fuses mended. New bottles of correcting fluid handed out . . . .'

'Mr Darke,' Lucy said, looking straight into his small, bright eyes, 'Who is Miss Broome?'

'Wrong question, Miss Beck.'

Lucy thought for a moment, then said, 'Who *was* Miss Broome?'

He beamed at her approvingly: 'You catch on quick, I'll say that for you. In fact, you're not the timid mouse you look, Miss Beck. You're a right little lion. Need to be, if you're going to take on Miss Broome. Tough old devil, she was.'

'Tell me about her,' Lucy said, as they sat over their tea.

'She was old Mr Bannister's secretary. Been here forty-three years, girl, woman and old misery. Sitting there where you're sitting now, her back straight as a ruler, and a chop-your-head-off ruler, too! Her stiff old fingers tapping out the letters one by one, with her nose nearly on the keyboard, so short-sighted she'd become by then.

None of your touch-typing for her! Every letter she stared in the face like it was a criminal and she the judge. You can't wonder she hates you young girls, with your fingers flying over the keys like white butterflies, and your eyes gazing out into the sunshine. They gave her the push, you know.'

'After forty-three years?' Lucy said, shocked into sympathy.

'Well, she was past it, wasn't she? Of course they wrapped it up in tissue paper. Gave her a brass clock and shook her hand and waved her goodbye. She didn't want to go. Didn't have anywhere worth going to – a bedsit, a gas ring. . . . The old bag didn't have any family who'd own her. This place was her home, this job was all she lived for.'

Lucy was silent. Her mother had turned Uncle Bert out once, after a row, shouting that she'd had enough of him. Six weeks later, she had asked him to come back. 'He looked so lonely, so lost,' she had told Lucy. 'All by himself in that horrid little room, with the worn lino and the curtains all shrunk.'

'Sorry for her, are you?' Harry Darke asked, watching her face.

Lucy hardened her heart.

'It's *my* job now,' she said. 'I need it. She can't have it for ever, it's not fair. It's my turn now.'

'So it's a fight to the finish, is it, Miss Beck?' he asked, smiling.

'Yes,' she said, and unscrewed the cap from the bottle of correcting fluid.

Her mother was working late that night. Lucy, going into the kitchen to get her own supper, was surprised to find the table neatly laid out with ham and salad, apple pie and a jug of tinned milk. Uncle Bert was sitting waiting for her, beaming proudly.

'Thought I'd have your supper ready,' he explained, 'now you're a working girl.'

'Thanks,' she said, but couldn't resist adding nastily, 'I don't get paid till Friday, you know. No good trying to touch me for a fiver.'

He flushed. 'You don't think much of me, do you? Who are you to set yourself up as judge and jury? You don't know what it's like . . . not being wanted. A little kindness would help!'

Lucy noticed his hands were shaking. His collapsing face seemed held together in a scarlet net of broken veins. His eyes were miserable.

'Uncle Bert . . . ' she began.

'What?' He looked at her warily.

'I'm sorry. I'm sorry, Uncle Bert.'

'I'm sorry, too, Lucy,' he said. 'I know it's a nuisance, having me here.'

'No! No, it isn't! We want you,' she said.

They smiled at each other timidly over the kitchen table, each remembering the little girl and the handsome uncle, who had once flown kites together in Waterlow Park.

Wednesday was Harry Darke's day off. Alone in the office, Lucy put a sheet of paper in the typewriter, and typed quickly:

QWERTYUIOPQWERTYUIOPQWERTYUIOP.

The typewriter gave a jerk, as if surprised, and hummed.

Lucy typed:

Dear Miss Broome,
Mr Darke told me you used to be secretary to Mr Bannister . . .
I AM, interrupted the typewriter.

Lucy went on,

> I am sorry to have to tell you that Mr Bannister [she hesitated, wondering how to put it,] . . . passed on three years ago, at the age of eighty-six . . .
> LIAR! I DON'T BELIEVE YOU!
> It is true, Miss Broome. I have seen his grave in the cemetery. It is not far from yours. I went along last night and left you flowers . . .
> ! ! ! ! !
> I did. Mr Darke is worried about Mr Bannister. He does not know how he will manage without you . . .
> HE CAN MANAGE WITHOUT ME ALL RIGHT! said the typewriter bitterly, HE TOLD ME TO GO. BRASS CLOCK, WHAT DID I WANT WITH BRASS CLOCKS! I WANTED MY JOB.
> They only asked you to go because they were worried about your health. [Lucy typed quickly.] Mr Darke told me Mr Bannister was always saying how much he missed you . . .
> ? ? ?
> Truly. He said Mr Bannister complained none of the new girls were any good. There was no one like you, he said . . . .

The typewriter was silent. Sunlight glittered on its keys, so that they looked wet.

> . . . He must miss you. He's probably in an awful muddle up there, mislaying his wings. Losing his harp. He needs someone to look after him . . .

The machine was silent. Lucy waited, but it said nothing more.

So she typed:

Goodbye, Miss Broome. Best of luck in your new
job,

Yours sincerely,
Lucy Beck, Secretary.

She folded the finished letter into a paper dart and sent
it sailing out of the window. The wind caught it and
carried it away.

Mr Ross is delighted now with his new secretary. Harry
Darke says she's champion and gives her chocolate
biscuits with her tea.
'However did you do it?' he asked.

William Darling
Anne Fine

It isn't even my real name, that's what gets me. I can see
that if I'd been *born* with a name like William Darling, if
it was written in great curly letters across my *birth*
certificate or something, then I might have to put up with
it. But it isn't even my proper name!

I had trouble from my first day at school. I was in more
fights than anyone Mrs Hurd could remember, and she'd
been teaching twenty years. It took weeks for some of
the people in my class to realize that, when they sidled
up and whispered, 'Hello, William Darling', I was going
to turn round and biff them. I don't like being teased
myself, and I certainly don't like to hear people teasing
my father.

Mind you, it's his own fault. He started it off. I'm sure
he didn't mean to cause me any trouble. It just worked
out that way. You see, my father's *terribly* old. His hair's
all silver, he gets arthritis in damp weather, and he uses
huge spotted cotton handkerchiefs, not paper tissues, to
blow his nose when he gets a cold. (He makes the most
extraordinary trumpeting noise. People look round.) He
had another family, all grown up before he even *thought*
of marrying my mother and starting on me. They drop in
every now and again, and it's so odd to think that they're
my half-brothers. They look old enough to be my father.
And my father looks old enough to be my grandpa.

And he's old-fashioned, too. He likes things like
starched sheets and fountain pens you fill from glass ink
bottles, and mealtimes so late that Mum and I have
practically starved to death before the food's even on
the table.

And he calls me William Darling.

He doesn't mean anything by it, I know. He doesn't *want* to make my life difficult. It's just he's too set in his ways to change.

He should have grown up at Wallisdean Primary School. He'd know a lot better then! He'd know that it's quite all right if your mother leans over the school fence and calls out, 'Hurry up, darling!' Nobody thinks twice about it. Nobody even seems to *hear*. But if your father does it, you're in big trouble – or a lot of fights.

Me, I was in a lot of fights. It took weeks before my father could stroll along to school with me in the morning and hand me my lunchbox, saying, 'There you are, darling,' without great choruses of sniggers breaking out all around me. I had to get tough with Melissa Halestrap for eight days in a row before she learned to stop lifting my coat off its hook at the end of the day and handing it to me with a really good imitation of my father's voice: 'Come along, William Darling. Button up. Freezy cold outside!'

No, it wasn't easy. I had to work at things at Wallisdean Primary. But I managed. And in the end I was perfectly satisfied and happy (and even Mrs Hurd admitted to my mum at the jumble sale in aid of the school roof that I'd stopped all that frightful fighting, and matured a lot). Then, suddenly, one day, the bombshell dropped.

'And when you move on to your next school in September . . . '

That's all Mrs Hurd said. (What I mean is, I was so shocked I didn't listen to the rest.) I'm not *stupid*. I knew I was in the school's oldest class. I knew we moved on. So I must have *realized* it was our last term at Wallisdean. It's just I hadn't realized how soon the change was. And, worse, it suddenly struck me that, just as I'd finally persuaded everybody in this school that it was a really bad idea to try and get away with calling me William Darling, I'd have to start all over again somewhere else.

And it would be even harder than before. Everyone would be older, and the older you get, the sillier William Darling sounds to you. And though I didn't know exactly what sort of teasing you'd get in the new school, I felt pretty sure of one thing: it would be worse.

I fretted about it, on and off, for the whole of the last two weeks of the term. And through the start of the summer holidays. Then, when I saw that worrying was spoiling everything, I reckoned I'd try tackling the matter head on. I thought it would be best.

'Please,' I said to my father. 'Since I'm starting at a new school, will you try to get out of the habit of calling me William Darling?'

He lowered his *Financial Times* and peered at me over it through the gold-rimmed half-moon spectacles he wears three-quarters of the way down his nose.

'Quite understand,' he told me. 'No problem, sweetheart.'

You can see why I wasn't optimistic. William Sweetheart is no better. And when, by the end of the week, he'd called me pumpkin, poppet, lambkin and muffin in his attempts to avoid the dreaded word, I just gave up.

Only three weeks to go. Have to try something else.

Sulking. I'd try sulking. I wouldn't answer him. If he called me William Darling, I'd go all fish-faced, and refuse to respond.

It didn't work, of course. He hates me being miserable. He hovered over me the entire week. 'What's the matter? Something up? Do tell. Oh, what a gloomy bird you are, darling!'

No luck there, then. And only two weeks to go. I was getting so desperate I thought I'd try bribery. I've found that bribery often works when all else fails.

'If I weed the whole garden,' I wheedled. 'Properly. Front *and* back. *And* down the side behind the garage. *And* along the verge – '

His spoon drifted to a halt halfway between his breakfast bowl of stewed prunes and his open mouth. One bushy silver eyebrow shot up. I thought he might be going to have a heart attack.

'If I do all that, will you stop calling me William Darling?'

'Of *course* I will, William, darling!'

'Starting right now!'

'Yes, d – ' He practically had to choke it back with the stewed prunes. 'Yes, William.' He practised it to himself sternly, several times, in between mouthfuls. 'Yes, William. Thank you, William. Oh, really, William? Quite so, William. Quite so.'

I left him chuntering, and strode out determinedly to the toolshed. I worked the whole day. I never stopped, except when Mum brought out a plate of sandwiches and shared them with me on the steps, admiring all the work I'd done, and helping me replant all the marigolds I'd pulled out of the ground by mistake.

At half-past five I finished the very last square millimetre of the verge. I waved triumphantly to Mum, and she went to fetch him.

They came back arm in arm. They strolled round the garden together as if the place were owned by the National Trust, praising everything, and gasping at how tidy it looked. Then he turned round and pressed a brand-new, shiny ten-pence piece into my hand. (He often does this. He's so old that he thinks ten pence is a fortune. It's one of the worst things about marrying someone a lot older than yourself, Mum says. You spend a fiver, and they think you're wicked.)

'Thank you,' I said, and put the coin in my pocket.

'Don't lose it,' he warned me.

Don't lose it! I get ten of them every week for pocket money. He must know that. But he's in the habit of keeping shiny coins he comes across in a special pocket in his waistcoat, ready to press them on the deserving, and he's too old to bother to change. So I held my tongue.

Pity he didn't.

'Splendid!' he said, waving to indicate my handiwork. 'You've done a beautiful job, William, darling!'

Mum tried to save the day. She spun him round and started pointing out how well the sweet peas were growing up the wall. But I was desperate. I'd slaved all day, and I'd got nowhere. I couldn't help it. I just lost my temper. Hurling the hoe down on the lawn, I yelled at him that I'd spent the *whole day* working because we'd made a *deal*, he'd *promised* me, and what happens? What's the very first thing he says? William Darling!

I threw my arms out, and wailed dramatically, 'What can I *do*? I'm not a baby any more! You've got to get out of the habit of calling me William Darling!'

It's always a bad move, losing your temper in front of anyone over fifty-five. They're old enough to think it's disgraceful.

'Listen to me, William,' he said. 'Manners like that simply will not do. I am extremely sorry that, so soon after our little agreement, the word happened to slip out. But tantrums are quite inexcusable. Pick up that hoe.'

I picked up that hoe.

'And kindly apologize to your mother.'

I muttered something that might, or might not, have been 'Sorry, Mum'. She didn't mind. She understood perfectly well how ratty I was getting about the whole business. *She* knew I wasn't a baby any more. *She* understood that things would be very different at the new school.

And maybe that's the reason she fixed up that arrangement the next day. Maybe that's why she made a special point of making my father take me into town shopping. 'He needs an awful lot of new stuff,' she said. 'You can take him.'

'Me? Why *me*?' (He hates shopping. He says the assistants are 'too big for their boots' and don't know the first thing about what they're selling. He nearly had a stroke last year when the girl in Woolies paused in the act of snipping the elastic thread Mum was buying, and asked how many centimetres there were in a metre. Mum pretends it was the girl's shocking mathematics that so upset him. But I know better. I know it was the fact that, until then, he hadn't realized yards, feet and inches have gone.)

'You have to take him,' Mum insisted. 'Because I'll be at work. And you're retired.'

No arguing with that. He had to take me.

He didn't enjoy it. First we went into Brierleys to buy an electronic calculator – not any old cheap one for beginners, but the sort my new school recommends, the Fz 753xb, which does all manner of fancy things I certainly hope I'll never need.

'Bit sophisticated, isn't it?' he said, inspecting the price sticker with even more interest than the calculator itself. 'For a child.'

The shop girl gave him a pretty cool look.

'Pretty sophisticated maths they do at this young man's age,' she retorted.

He looked around for the young man, and was a bit put out just to see me.

'Hrrrumph,' he said. But he wrote out the cheque, and signed it with his extraordinary flourish.

Then we went to Skinners to buy football boots. As soon as they found a pair that fitted me, he handed over the cheque he'd been filling out while I was lacing up.

'Eight pounds, twenty,' he said.

She shook her head and handed the cheque back to him with the neatly written bill.

'Twelve pounds, ten pence,' she corrected him. 'Your boy is in the large foot range now.'

Without saying a word, he tore the first cheque into tiny pieces. Then, still without speaking, he wrote out another.

He was in quite a mood by the time we reached Hilliards to buy my new blazer. He strode straight over to the rack which had the smallest sizes hanging from it, and had to be steered to the taller rack behind, where all the larger (and more expensive) ones hung.

'Bit pricey,' he complained.

'Wait till he shoots up,' said the shop assistant. 'He'll grow out of a blazer a week!'

My father looked horrified. When he wrote the cheque, his hand was trembling. It can't be easy for a man who still thinks that ten pence is wealth.

He claimed that he needed some time to recover.

'Bills, bills, bills!' he groused. 'Let's go and have a cup of tea while the feeling returns to my cheque-signing fingers.'

He chose the same old teashop we've gone to for years. (Mum says they bought their first high chair for me.) We took our usual table, and my father gave the usual order to the new summer waitress.

'One lightly buttered toasted teacake, and a Balloon Special.'

(Maybe I should tell you that, with a Balloon Special, you get three flavours of ice-cream, and a big red balloon tied to the back of your chair.)

The waitress gave me a suspicious look.

'He looks a bit old for a Balloon Special,' she said. 'It's only supposed to be for sevens and under.' (She was so new, she still remembered the rules.)

'Really?' said my father frostily. 'Then *two* lightly buttered toasted teacakes.'

I didn't argue. I suddenly reckoned I understood why Mum had been so keen to send us off together. She wanted him to realize for himself I wasn't a baby any longer. I did hard maths. I had big feet. If I'd grown out of big red balloons and into teacakes, maybe I'd also grown out of being called William Darling.

I wasn't his darling right now, that was for sure. He was flicking back through the chequebook.

'Bills, bills, bills!' he grumbled. 'You're costing me a fortune. I ought to call you "bill"!'

The waitress sailed over with the teacakes.

'One for me,' said my father. 'And one for "bill" here.'

She laid the teacakes down without so much as a flicker of her eyebrows. She obviously thought what he said sounded perfectly normal.

And so it did, of course – bill-William-Bill!

I couldn't believe my luck. The joke amused him so much, he kept it up all the way home: 'Tired, bill?' and all through the evening: 'Nice mug of hot chocolate, bill?' and at bedtime: 'Cleaned your teeth, bill?' The joke ran for *weeks*. Sometimes I worried that he might be on the verge of finding it boring, but I'd just leave out my calculator, or my blazer, or my new football boots, and he'd be off again: 'Getting ready for school, bill?'

And to my amazement, the joke was still making him chuckle right through the last days of the holiday, and the parents' evening. Grinning, my father introduced me to my new form teacher.

'This is my bill,' he said.

Mr Henry looked at me.

'Hello, Bill.'

That was all he said!

And it went on that way. I couldn't believe my good fortune was holding. When I walked in the classroom on the first morning, all Mr Henry said was, 'Here, Bill. These books are for you,' and by break everybody just called me Bill as if I'd never in my life been William Darling.

I stayed Bill all through lunch, and all afternoon. I stayed Bill all week – no fuss, no fights. Mrs Hurd would have been astonished. She wouldn't have known me. I worried sometimes, quite a lot, because I knew I couldn't keep my father away from the school grounds for ever, but then I'd put the anxiety out of my mind, and just enjoy things.

And then, this afternoon, it finally happened. Our class was playing football on the pitch, when suddenly I caught sight of my father's straw boater sailing along on the other side of the school hedge. I kept my head down, dreading the moment I just *knew* was coming the instant he reached the gap at the gate, glanced in, and saw me. Chills ran down my spine. My knees were shaking. Did I have time to run off the pitch?

Too late! Over the gate I heard his clear, clear voice.

'Go for it, William, darling! Boot that ball!'

The football was sailing down towards me, head on. Swinging my foot back, I booted it as hard as I could, *really* hard, as if to let the teasers know, right from the very start, what I could do.

The ball flew down the pitch in a perfect arc.

Then I looked round. No teasers? Mr Henry called out, 'Well done, Bill!' as he puffed past, but no one else was paying the slightest attention. No one was even looking my way. They'd all gone haring up the field after the ball, and I suddenly realized that no one had, even for a single moment, connected me with that silvery-haired (and probably confused) old gentleman who yelled encouragement over the fence, and then strolled on.

William Darling? No. No William Darling in this game, I'm afraid. Me? Oh, my name's Bill.

The Bakerloo Flea
Michael Rosen

Not long ago I was in a pub round the Elephant and
Castle, and I got talking to a woman, an oldish woman.
And we were talking about this and that, and she said she
used to be a cleaner down the Underground. I didn't
know, but it seems as if every night after the last tube,
they switch the electric current off and teams of night-
cleaners go through the Underground, along the tunnels,
cleaning up all the muck, rubbish, fag-ends and stuff that
we chuck on to the lines. They sweep out between the
lines on one station, and then, in a gang of about six
or seven, walk on to the next station along the lines in
the tunnels.

Anyway this woman (I don't know her name), she says
to me:

'Did you ever hear talk of the Bakerloo flea?'

'Bakerloo flea?' I said. 'No, no, never.'

'Well,' she said, 'you know there are rats down there –
down the Underground? Hundreds of 'em. And the thing
is,' she said, 'is that some of them have grown enormous.
Huge great big things.'

'I've heard of them,' I said. 'Super rats.'

'Right,' she says. 'Now you tell me,' she says, 'what lives
on rats? Fleas, right? Fleas. So – the bigger the rats the
bigger the fleas. Stands to reason. These rats, they feed
on all the old garbage that people throw down on the
lines. It's amazing what people throw away, you know.'

She told me they found a steak down there once,
lipstick, a bowler hat, beads, a box of eggs and hundreds
and hundreds of sweets – especially Maltesers and those
balls of bubble gum you get out of slot machines.

Anyway, the rats eat these, get big and it seems that one day they were working the Bakerloo Line – Elephant and Castle to Finchley Road – and just before Baker Street one of the women in the gang was looking ahead, and she screamed out:

'Look – look – what's that?' Up in front was a great, grey, spiky thing with huge hairy legs and big jaws. It was as big as a big dog – bigger.

And the moment she screamed, it jumped away from them, making a sort of grating, scraping noise. Well, they were scared stiff. Scared stiff. But they had to finish the job, so they carried on up the line to Finchley Road. But they didn't see it again that night or the next, or the next.

Some of them thought they'd imagined it, because it can get very spooky down there. They sing and shout a lot she told me, and tell saucy jokes, not fit for my ears.

Anyway, about a fortnight later, at the same place – just before Baker Street on the Bakerloo Line – suddenly one of them looks up and there it was again. A great, big, grey, spiky thing with long legs and big jaws.

'It's a flea, sure to God it's a flea,' one of them said.

The moment it heard this, again it jumped. Again, they heard this scraping, grating sound, and it disappeared down the tunnel – in the dark. They walked on, Baker Street, St Johns Wood, Swiss Cottage, to Finchley Road. Nothing.

Anyway – this time they had a meeting. They decided it *was* a flea, a gigantic flea, and it must have grown up from a family of fleas that had lived for years and years growing bigger and bigger, sucking the blood of all the fat rats down there.

So they decided that it was time to tell one of the high-ups in London Transport, or they wouldn't go down there any more.

For a start off, no one'd believe them.

'Just a gang of women seeing things in the dark,' the supervisor said.

Right! One of them had a bright idea. She said:

'I'll tell you what we'll do – we'll tell them that we're coming out on strike, and we'll tell the papers about the flea, the Bakerloo flea. It'll be a huge scandal – no one'll dare go by tube, it'll be a national scandal.'

So they threatened the manager with this, and this time the high-ups really moved. They were so scared the story might get out, and they'd be blamed and one of *them* would lose their jobs.

So for a start they stopped all cleaning on the Bakerloo Line, and one of the high-ups went down the tunnel with the women. You can just see it, can't you? Four in the morning, a gang of six women with feather dusters, and one of the bowler hat and briefcase brigade walking down the tunnel on the hunt for the Bakerloo flea. Sounded incredible to me.

Anyway, it seems as if they came round that same corner just before Baker Street and the women had gone quiet and the bloke was saying: 'If this is a hoax, if this is a trick . . . ' when they heard that awful, hollow, scraping noise.

At first they couldn't see it, but then – there it was – not *between* the lines this time – *on* the lines – a gigantic flea. No question, that's what it was.

Well, he took one look at it, and next moment he was backing off.

'Back, ladies, back. Back, ladies!'

Of course *he* was more scared than they were. Terrified. But he was even more terrified when one of the women let out this scream. Not because *she* was scared, but to scare off the flea. And it worked. It jumped. Right out of sight.

Well there was no carrying on up the line that night.

'Back, ladies, back,' was all he could say, and back they went.

Next thing they knew, they were all called into an office with a carpet and the Queen on the wall. And there was a whole gang of these men.

First thing, one of them says, they weren't to let anyone know of this, no one at all must ever hear of what they had all seen. There was no point in letting a panic develop. Anyway, next he says:

'We haven't let the grass grow under our feet. We've got a scientist with us.'

And then the scientist, he says:

'I've got this powder. Deadly flea powder. All you need to do is spread this up and down the Bakerloo Line, and there's be no more trouble with this flea thing.'

Well, the woman in the pub – I never found out her name – said:

'So who's going to spread this stuff about down there? The Army?'

'No,' the man said. 'We don't see any need for that. 'You,' he says, 'you.'

'So that's a fine one,' the woman said to me. 'First of all they said it was just a bunch of women afraid of the dark, then they send Tarzan in pinstripes down there and he can't get out fast enough, and now it's us that has to spread this flea powder.'

'Well,' she said, 'we knew it wouldn't be any good anyway. Flea powder never is.'

They took it down there, threw it about between Regent's Park and Baker Street and Swiss Cottage – while up above, in the big houses, ambassadors from all over the world slept soundly in their beds. They told them not to go down for a week, and not to breathe a word of it to anyone.

'They were more scared of a story in the papers than we were of the flea,' she said.

It hadn't attacked anyone, no one had seen it there in daytime, so down they went. But there it was again – sitting there just before Baker Street, with some of the powder sticking to the hairs on its legs. But this time, instead of hopping away down the line, it turned and faced them. They turned and ran, and then it leaped. It leaped at the women, and they ran back down the tunnel to Regent's Park. This great, grey flea was trying to get at them.

'We screamed,' she said, 'we really screamed, but it was after us, 'cos you see that damned flea powder hadn't killed the flea – it had killed the rats. It was starving for fresh blood. Probably *mad* for blood, by now,' she said. 'We ran and ran and the flea was hopping – but it was hitting the roof of the tunnel, it was so mad to get at us. There was this terrible scraping sound of its shell on the roof of the tunnel, and it'd fall back on to the lines. So we could move faster than it. We rushed back to Regent's Park, and calls went up and down the line and all over the system to lock the gates on every station and seal the system. Seal off the Underground system of London. Well, it was about four o'clock – two hours to go before a million people would be down there.

'What were they going to do? Upstairs in the office they were in a blind panic. They could've done something about it earlier, instead of fobbing us off. They couldn't call in the Army without telling the Minister, and if they told the Minister, he'd tell the Prime Minister, and all the high-ups would get the sack. So they had this plan to turn the current on, and run the maintenance train at high speed through the tunnel from Finchley Road to the Elephant and Castle, in the hope that it would get killed

beneath the wheels of the train, or smashed against the buffers at the Elephant.

'They did it. They sent it through. Of course *that* didn't work. We knew it wouldn't work. Anyone that's lived with a flea knows you can't squash fleas – you've got to crack 'em. They're hard, rock hard.'

'After the maintenance man ran the maintenance train through, they went down to the gates at Regent's Park, and they stood and listened, and from down below they could hear the grating, scraping noise of its shell on its legs. Of course, it was obvious now why it had stuck to this stretch of the line all the time. Some of the juiciest rubbish was in the bins round those posh parts, so you got the biggest rats, so that was where you got the great Bakerloo flea.

'So now they had less than two hours to get rid of the flea, or leave it for a day and run the risk of letting a million people down into the tunnels to face a flea, starving, starving for blood, or shutting the whole system down and telling everyone to go by bus.

'Well you know what happened?' she said. 'We did it. We got rid of it.'

'You did?'

'Yes, we did it.'

'Vera's old man worked on the dustcarts for Camden Council. She knew how to kill the flea. It was Vera's plan that what we'd do was go down, actually down on to the line at Oxford Circus with dustbin lids, banging them with brushes and broom handles, and drive the flea back up the line to Finchley Road where the Bakerloo Line comes out of the tunnel into the open air. And at Finchley Road, Vera's old man and his gang would have a couple of carts backed up into the tunnel. And that's what we did. We got driven to Vera's place to get her old man up, on to his mates' places to get them up, then they went to the

Council builder's yard to get boards, builders' planks. We got the lids off the bins and down we went. Oxford Circus, Regent's Park, Baker Street, St John's Wood, Swiss Cottage, Finchley Road, and we shouted and we banged, and we banged and we shouted every step of the way.

'We saw it just once at Swiss Cottage waiting for us, but we walked together holding the lids up in front of us like shields, and it was as if it knew it couldn't get at us this time, 'cos it turned – it had just room to turn in the tunnel – and as we came up to Finchley Road still banging and shouting, it leaped – not at us, but at one of the carts. Alongside it was the other one, between the wheels were the boards, some of them stacked up to block off all the gaps. The flea was trapped between us with our lids and the back of the dustcarts. It leaped, it hit the roof of the tunnel, just like it did when it chased us. We shouted and banged. It leaped again. This time we had it. It was in the back of the dustcart.

We kept up the banging and the shouting. We got as near to the back of the dustcart as we could. We could see it there, every hair of its legs, and Vera shouts:

'"Turn it on, Bob, turn it on," and Bob turned on the masher (they call it 'The Shark'), in the back of his cart. And it bit into the back of that flea like giant nails crunching through eggshells. The smell was revolting. Bit by bit, the flea was dragged into the cart. We could see it as it went: first its body, then its legs. I'll never forget the sight of those huge hairy legs twitching about in the back of Bob's cart, Vera shouting:

'"You've got him, love, you've got him!"

'He had, too. That was that. That was the end of the Bakerloo flea. But do you know, when we got up to the top, that load from head office were there. They were crying, crying out of relief, crying their eyes out. Twenty minutes later, hundreds and thousands of people were down there, off to work, none the wiser. They didn't know about any flea, any Bakerloo flea. They don't even know we go down there every night cleaning up their mess for them. Of course, head office made us promise never to breathe a word of it. We promised.

'Vera said:

'"What's it worth to you?"

'He said:

'"Your honour. Your word. And your word's your honour."

'And they gave us a week's extra holiday tagged on to August Bank Holiday that year.'

She told me I was the first person she'd ever told the story to, and told me never to tell anyone. The scandal would be terrible. I don't know whether to believe her or not.

The Stowaways
Roger McGough

When I lived in Liverpool, my best friend was a boy called
Midge. Kevin Midgeley was his 'real name, but we
called him Midge for short. And he was short, only
about three cornflake packets high (empty ones at that).
No three ways about it. Midge was my best friend and we
had lots of things in common. Things we enjoyed doing
like . . . climbing trees, playing footy, going to the
pictures, hitting each other really hard. And there
were things we didn't enjoy doing like . . . sums,
washing behind our ears, eating cabbage.

But there was one thing that really bound us together,
one thing we had in common – a love of the sea.

In the old days (but not so long ago) the River Mersey
was far busier than it is today. Those were the days of the
great passenger liners and cargo boats. Large ships sailed
out of Liverpool for Canada, the United States, South
Africa, the West Indies, all over the world. My father had
been to sea and so had all my uncles, and my grandfather.
Six foot six, muscles rippling in the wind, huge hands
grappling with the helm, rum-soaked and fierce as a
wounded shark (and that was only my grandmother!). By
the time they were twenty, most young men in this city
had visited parts of the globe I can't even spell.

In my bedroom each night, I used to lie in bed (best
place to lie really), I used to lie there, especially in
winter, and listen to the foghorns being sounded all
down the river. I could picture the ship nosing its way
out of the docks into the channel and out into the Irish
Sea. It was exciting. All those exotic places. All those
exciting adventures.

Midge and I knew what we wanted to do when we left school . . . become sailors. A captain, an admiral, perhaps one day even a steward. Of course we were only about seven or eight at the time so we thought we'd have a long time to wait. But oddly enough, the call of the sea came sooner than we'd expected.

It was a Wednesday if I remember rightly. I never liked Wednesdays for some reason. I could never spell it for a start and it always seemed to be raining, and there were still two days to go before the weekend. Anyway, Midge and I got into trouble at school. I don't remember what for (something trivial I suppose like chewing gum in class, forgetting how to read, setting fire to the music teacher), I forget now. But we were picked on, nagged, told off and all those boring things that grown-ups get up to sometimes.

And, of course, to make matters worse, my mum and dad were in a right mood when I got home. Nothing to do with me, of course, because as you have no doubt gathered by now, I was the perfect child: clean, well-mannered, obedient . . . soft in the head. But for some reason I was clipped round the ear and sent to bed early for being childish. Childish! I ask you. I *was* a child. A child acts his age, what does he get? Wallop!

So that night in bed, I decided . . . Yes, you've guessed it. I could hear the big ships calling out to each other as they sidled out of the Mersey into the oceans beyond. The tugs leading the way like proud little guide dogs. That's it. We'd run away to sea, Midge and I. I'd tell him the good news in the morning.

The next two days just couldn't pass quickly enough for us. We had decided to begin our amazing around-the-world voyage on Saturday morning so that in case we didn't like it we would be back in time for school on Monday. As you can imagine there was a lot to think about – what clothes to take, how much food and drink. We decided on two sweaters each and wellies in case we ran into storms around Cape Horn. I read somewhere that sailors lived off rum and dry biscuits, so I poured some of my dad's into an empty pop bottle, and borrowed a handful of half-coated chocolate digestives. I also packed my lonestar cap gun and Midge settled on a magnifying glass.

On Friday night we met round at his house to make the final plans. He lived with his granny and his sister, so there were no nosy parents to discover what we were up to. We hid all the stuff in the shed in the yard and arranged to meet outside his back door next morning at the crack of dawn, or sunrise – whichever came first.

Sure enough, Saturday morning, when the big finger was on twelve and the little one was on six, Midge and I met with our little bundles under our arms and ran up the street as fast as our tiptoes could carry us.

Hardly anyone was about, and the streets were so quiet and deserted except for a few pigeons straddling home after all-night parties. It was a very strange feeling, as if we were the only people alive and the city belonged entirely to us. And soon the world would be ours as well – once we'd stowed away on a ship bound for somewhere far off and exciting.

By the time we'd got down to the Pier Head, though, a lot more people were up and about, including a policeman who eyed us suspiciously. 'Ello, Ello, Ello,' he said, 'and where are you two going so early in the morning?'

'Fishing,' I said.

'Train spotting,' said Midge and we looked at each other.

'Just so long as you're not running away to sea.'

'Oh no,' we chorused. 'Just as if.'

He winked at us. 'Off you go then, and remember to look both ways before crossing your eyes.'

We ran off and straight down on to the landing-stage where a lot of ships were tied up. There was no time to lose because already quite a few were putting out to sea, their sirens blowing, the hundreds of seagulls squeaking excitedly, all tossed into the air like giant handfuls of confetti.

Then I noticed a small ship just to the left where the crew were getting ready to cast off. They were so busy doing their work that it was easy for Midge and me to slip on board unnoticed. Up the gang-plank we went and straight up on to the top deck where there was nobody around. The sailors were all busy down below, hauling in the heavy ropes and revving up the engine that turned the great propellers.

We looked around for somewhere to hide. 'I know, let's climb down the funnel,' said Midge.

'Great idea,' I said, taking the mickey. 'Or, better still, let's disguise ourselves as a pair of seagulls and perch up there on the mast.'

Then I spotted them. The lifeboats. 'Quick, let's climb into one of those, they'll never look in there – not unless we run into icebergs anyway.' So in we climbed, and no sooner had we covered ourselves with the tarpaulin than there was a great shuddering and the whole ship seemed to turn round on itself. We were off! Soon we'd be digging for diamonds in the Brazilian jungle or building sand-castles on a tropical island. But we had to be patient, we knew that. Those places are a long way away, it could takes days, even months.

So we were patient. Very patient. Until after what seemed like hours and hours we decided to eat our rations, which I divided up equally. I gave Midge all the rum and I had all the biscuits. Looking back on it now, that probably wasn't a good idea, especially for Midge.

What with the rolling of the ship and not having had any breakfast, and the excitement, and couple of swigs of rum – well you can guess what happened – woooorrppp! All over the place. We pulled back the sheet and decided to give ourselves up. We were too far away at sea now for the captain to turn back. The worst he could do was to clap us in irons or shiver our timbers.

We climbed down on to the deck and as Midge staggered to the nearest rail to feed the fishes, I looked out to sea hoping to catch sight of a whale, a shoal of dolphins, perhaps see the coast of America coming in to view. And what did I see? The Liver Buildings.

Anyone can make a mistake can't they? I mean, we weren't to know we'd stowed away on a ferryboat.

One that goes from Liverpool to Birkenhead and back again, toing and froing across the Mersey. We'd done four trips hidden in the lifeboat and ended up back in Liverpool. And we'd only been away about an hour and a half. 'Ah well, so much for running away to sea,' we thought as we disembarked (although disembowelled might be a better word as far as Midge was concerned). Rum? Yuck.

We got the bus home. My mum and dad were having their breakfast. 'Aye, aye,' said my dad, 'here comes the early bird. And what have you been up to then?'

'I ran away to sea,' I said.

'Mm, that's nice,' said my mum, shaking out the cornflakes. 'That's nice.'

Pete Johnson The Protectors
Jennifer Johnston Shadows on Our Skin
Geraldine Kaye Comfort Herself
Daniel Keyes Flowers for Algernon
Dick King-Smith The Sheep-Pig
Elizabeth Laird Red Sky in the Morning; Kiss the Dust
D H Lawrence The Fox and The Virgin and the Gypsy; Selected Tales
George Layton The Swap
Harper Lee To Kill a Mockingbird
C Day Lewis The Otterbury Incident
Joan Lingard Across the Barricades; The File on Fraulein Berg
Penelope Lively The Ghost of Thomas Kempe
Jack London The Call of the Wild; White Fang
Bernard MacLaverty Cal; The Best of Bernard Mac Laverty
James Vance Marshall Walkabout
Ian McEwan The Daydreamer; A Child in Time
Michael Morpurgo My Friend Walter; The Wreck of the Zanzibar;
The War of Jenkins' Ear; Why the Whales Came; Arthur, High King
of Britain; Kensuke's Kingdom; Hereabout Hill
Beverley Naidoo No Turning Back
Bill Naughton The Goalkeeper's Revenge
New Windmill A Charles Dickens Selection
New Windmill Book of Classic Short Stories
New Windmill Book of Fiction and Non-fiction: Taking Off!
New Windmill Book of Haunting Tales
New Windmill Book of Humorous Stories: Don't Make Me Laugh
New Windmill Book of Nineteenth Century Short Stories
New Windmill Book of Non-fiction: Get Real!
New Windmill Book of Non-fiction: Real Lives, Real Times
New Windmill Book of Scottish Short Stories
New Windmill Book of Short Stories: Fast and Curious
New Windmill Book of Short Stories: From Beginning to End
New Windmill Book of Short Stories: Into the Unknown
New Windmill Book of Short Stories: Tales with a Twist
New Windmill Book of Short Stories: Trouble in Two Centuries
New Windmill Book of Short Stories: Ways with Words
New Windmill Book of Short Stories by Women
New Windmill Book of Stories from many Cultures and Traditions:
Fifty-Fifty Tutti-Frutti Chocolate-Chip
New Windmill Book of Stories from Many Genres: Myths, Murders
and Mysteries

How many have you read?